# FOR Chiefs Fans ONLY

## 50 Years of Moments, Memories, and Milestones That Made Us Love Our Team

By Bill Althaus and Rich Wolfe

Foreword by Chiefs Greats, Players, Coaches, and Fans

ASCEND BOOKS

www.ascendbooks.com

Requests for permission should be addressed to Ascend Books, LLC, Attn: Rights and Permissions Department

10 9 8 7 6 5 4 3 2 1

Printed in the United States of America

ISBN-13: 978-0-9817166-7-1
ISBN-10: 0-9817166-7-9

Library of Congress Cataloging-in-Publications Data Available Upon Request

Editor: Lee Stuart

Design: Randy Lackey, The Covington Group

Cover photo courtesy of Scott E. Thomas Photography

Back cover photo of Steve Gildehaus courtesy of Steve Gildehaus

This book is not an official publication of, nor is it endorsed by, the Kansas City Chiefs.

ASCEND BOOKS

www.ascendbooks.com

# FOR
## Chiefs Fans
### ONLY

## 50 Years of Moments, Memories, and Milestones That Made Us Love Our Team

# Special Thanks to Our Sponsors:

# Table of Contents

# Foreword
## *A Collection of Favorite Memories from Chiefs Fans*

*I was sitting in the Arrowhead Stadium parking lot, tailgating with my friends, when I see a golf cart with a couple of men coming toward my bus. I look a little bit closer and see that Lamar Hunt and Jack Steadman are in the golf cart. Mr. Hunt gets out and asks, "Where's Steve Gildehaus?" I was shocked. I didn't know what to think. I told him that I was Steve Gildehaus and he spent the next 45 minutes talking with me about the team, eating a hot dog or hamburger and having a soda. The girls in the office arranged everything because my bus had been voted the "Best of Show" for two years in a row. I am more than a fan. I guess you could call me a fanatic. We've been going to all the games for about 20 years – and we'll keep going another 20 years, God willing. They're the greatest show in town."*

**- STEVE GILDEHAUS**
**The Grain Valley developer, philanthropist and season ticket holder who owns the "Best of Show" game bus that was a favorite of late Kansas City Chiefs owner Lamar Hunt.**

*I love football, especially game day at Arrowhead Stadium. I played professional baseball, but football is the sport I love. I love to watch it, and I almost played it in college. I've been to just about every NFL stadium in the country and I love Green Bay and Lambeau Field. It's like the home of football. But for a game-day experience, the tailgating, and enjoying a great experience, it's tough to beat Arrowhead Stadium.*

**- BRIAN McRAE**
**Former all-state defensive back at Blue Springs High School and No. 1 draft pick of the Kansas City Royals, who went on to star for the Chicago Cubs and New York Mets.**

*So many things have changed about the game of professional football since I played. We used to have 32 players on a team. Now, they have 32 coaches. We were a close group, on and off the field. We did everything together and most of us got jobs in the off-season because we had families to support. But the one thing that has not changed is the atmosphere at Arrowhead Stadium. Back at old Municipal Stadium, the better we got, the louder it got. But at Arrowhead Stadium, my goodness, you can't talk to someone standing right next to you. It's the most amazing thing I have ever experienced on a football field – as a player or a spectator.*

**- BOBBY BELL**
**Kansas City Chiefs Hall of Fame linebacker.**

*There is something special about Arrowhead Stadium. When I walked into it the first time, I could smell the barbeque – and it smelled wonderful. We'd walk from our car to the stadium and smell that barbeque and I knew what all those television announcers were talking about all those years. It's something you have to experience. And then, you get inside the stadium and see that sea of red. It's just amazing.*

**- KEVIN COSTNER**
**Actor, writer, director, producer, and longtime Kansas City Chiefs football fan who loved Lenny the Cool Dawson and the Chiefs when he was growing up in Southern California.**

*I went to my first Chiefs game in 1979 against the Denver Broncos and it was about 13 degrees below zero and I was hooked. I loved the atmosphere. I loved everything about the game. Since that game, I've only missed two home games and look forward to everything about the game-day experience.*

**- MIKE EBENROTH**
**President of the Kansas City Chiefs Red Coaters.**

Len Dawson
Photo courtesy of Scott E. Thomas Photography

*Game day at Arrowhead Stadium is so special for me. When I played at Purdue, we never had a game with 78,000 people. When we started winning, we had 32,000 fans at Municipal Stadium, but the first time I walked into Arrowhead Stadium – for our first game against the Miami Dolphins since we'd moved from Municipal – it took my breath away looking out and seeing the stands filled with all those fans wearing Chiefs red and gold. Back when we first played at Arrowhead, our bench was on the north side of the field, the sun side. People asked us why we would be over there in the sun when it was 110 degrees in the shade early in the season. That's back when they shot all the games for television with the cameras in the press box and Hank wanted us to be on that side of the field where they would shoot our faces instead of our backsides. That was Hank Stram, and that was a special time to be a part of Arrowhead Stadium.*

**- LEN DAWSON**
**Kansas City Chiefs Hall of Fame quarterback.**

*That Monday Night Football Game against Buffalo was remarkable. The entire stadium was shaking. I've never been in a louder stadium. That was the night "Oh, baby, what a play!" was born. When I think back to the great nights of covering football and broadcasting games for the Kansas City Chiefs, they don't get much better than that. And the fans – those wonderful Kansas City Chiefs fans – had a lot to do with it.*

**- KEVIN HARLAN**
**Former Kansas City Chiefs broadcaster, who now covers the NFL for Fox Sports.**

*It is the loudest stadium in the country. I've been to a lot of NFL games, and no place compares to Arrowhead Stadium.*

**- GEORGE BRETT**
**Kansas City Royals Hall of Fame third baseman and a Kansas City Chiefs season ticket holder.**

*I remember sitting in the stands back in the late 70s and early 80s when there were about 7,000 people. I tell that to people now and they don't believe it. I think most fans today think that Arrowhead always was full, and it wasn't. I remember a game from the 13-3 season when we were in the parking lot and a big U-Haul parked right next to us. When they parked, a bunch of high school kids got out and they brought out a couch and set up a space in the parking lot like a living room. They told us they didn't have tickets, they just wanted to come out and experience the tailgating and the game-day experience. I never forgot that. I thought to myself, this place must be pretty special when kids want to come and sit in the parking lot just to experience what we get to experience every Sunday during the season.*

**- TERESA CLUM**
**Kansas City Chiefs season ticket holder.**

*Back in the day, the louder the stadium got, the better we played. During that Monday Night Game against Buffalo we fed off the fans. I get goose bumps just thinking about that game. That must have been what it was like to have played for the team during the glory years. We've had our ups and downs, but the fans always stood behind us. They are the best fans in the NFL. Period!*

**- BILL MAAS**
**Former All-Pro nose tackle who had two sacks in the memorable Monday Night Football win over Buffalo.**

*I was in the stands having a good time with all the Cowboy fans when the Chiefs played at Dallas, when someone came up and tapped me on the back. I turned around and it was Lamar Hunt. He'd seen me from his suite in the stadium and came down to talk to me. I couldn't believe it. I've been a fan for such a long time that I saw the Super Bowl parade in downtown Kansas City. I wanted to skip school and go to the parade, so I told the nurse I was sick. She didn't believe me. She told me I was going to the parade. Well, she was right. But I ran out of her office and all the time while I was at the parade I was afraid the cops were going to arrest me.*

**- MONTE SHORT**
**Arrowman, who wears the jersey of an opposing player filled with arrows. He was the first fan from Kansas City to be inducted into the Pro Football Hall of Fame.**

*This is home. This is where I want to be on a Sunday morning. There's nothing better than sharing Arrowhead Stadium with 78,000 of your noisiest friends.*

**- DERRICK THOMAS**
**The late, great linebacker of the Kansas City Chiefs who is the newest member of the team to be inducted into the Pro Football Hall of Fame.**

*When the Chiefs first came to town, you could have shot a shotgun into the stands at Municipal Stadium and no one would have gotten hurt because there weren't any people in the stands. But Mr. Hunt believed, and he built a great team, and look at 'em today – 80,000 a game.*

**- BOB JOHNSON**
**The colorful former rodeo cowboy who rode the team mascot, Warpaint, from 1963 to 1988 on the sidelines at Arrowhead Stadium.**

*My first seat was in the main part of the stadium, and we were pretty much protected from the elements. It used to snow back then at games, and it was nice to have the cover for protection. Then, they brought in those bleachers in left field of the baseball stadium and called it the Wolf Pack. My wife and I got seats out there and we were right next to War Paint – the horse that ran around the stadium after the Chiefs scored. I loved to watch that horse, and his rider had a war bonnet. I think they kept him out at Benjamin Stables. He was probably the most famous horse in the AFL. There were some great games, but the one I bet everyone talks about is the Christmas Day game in 1970. It was the longest game ever played and we had a lot of chances to win that game, but Miami came out on top with a field goal in the second overtime. I still love the Chiefs, but back then, we lived and died with them. It took a long time to get over that loss. That was the last game played in Municipal Stadium. The next year the team moved to Arrowhead and it was something to see. We all wondered where our seats would be in the new stadium and we were happy to see that they were three rows from the field right behind the Chiefs bench.*

**- ALTON WILLIFORD**
**Now 85, Williford was an original Kansas City Chiefs season ticket holder.**

*Game day at Arrowhead Stadium is like Christmas, Thanksgiving, and the Fourth of July all rolled into one big holiday. There's nothing like Arrowhead Stadium when it is packed with Chiefs fans. And they are the best fans in the world. Being a part of the Chiefs family for all those many years is something I will always treasure.*

**- TONY DiPARDO**
**The 97-year-old former bandleader of the Kansas City Chiefs, who worked 55 years on a handshake with team founder Lamar Hunt.**

# The Innovator and Founder

Lamar Hunt, the founder of the Chiefs and one of the members of the "Foolish Club" that created the American Football League, was regarded as an innovator and a pioneer in modern professional sports.

This section chronicles his story from the "original dream" to his induction into the Pro Football Hall of Fame.

*"Lamar Hunt was one of the giants of sports in America and the NFL, in particular. A chronicle of his contributions could fill two books."*

Sponsored by

## Sprint

# Lamar Hunt:
## The Father of the
## American Football League

*Lamar Hunt had a dream and he followed it, forming the American Football League. He later served as the founding father of the Dallas Texans and Kansas City Chiefs. The late Chiefs founder – he never really enjoyed being called the team's owner – sat down and wrote his own account of what it was like to start the American Football League. Here, in Hunt's own words, is that account:*

How did the AFL start? You never think of a light bulb coming on, but that was it, exactly, just like an old cartoon. The light just clicked on and got brighter and brighter.

It occurred to me, "Hey, what would be the possibility of putting together a second league?" I had had a number of conversations with the Wolfners; Mrs. Wolfner owned the Chicago Cardinals team. In the course of these conversations, they ultimately agreed to sell 20 percent of the team, but they didn't want it to move out of Chicago. They would let me have an option that if they ever moved, that they would move to Dallas.

It really wasn't something I wanted to do. In the course of the conversation they had mentioned many individuals' names. Did I know Bud Adams in Houston, Bob Howsam in Denver, Max Winter or Bill Boyer in Minneapolis?

It turns out, these were all people who had come to them about buying the Cardinals and moving them to their town. I thought about those people, and that's when the light bulb went off. If all of those people are interested, why not get them all together and form a league?

Never had a turndown. Knowing what I know now, I would expect some turndowns. The original six people we approached, no one turned us down.

We were called the "Foolish Club." Wayne Valley came up with that one day. He said, "This is a really foolish group. We ought to call ourselves the Foolish Club." He said he was going to start calling us the Foolish Club. Soon, everyone started calling ourselves that.

When the league was announced, I was a few days away from 27. If I knew what I know now, I would be on the beach at Waikiki, and not involved in a league. It was a different time and a different era. Now, there are so many things that have gone on in sports expansion. Teams failing. The ABA, the WHA League, even some of the NHL is failing. Obviously, there was the WFL. That was a very naive time, that it would be fairly easy to start a new league, that if it would succeed in Pittsburgh, Cleveland and Washington, why won't it succeed in Dallas, Houston and Denver? What made the AFL different from the ABA, WHA, WFL? I think we were an idea whose time was right.

Football had come into a success era – the NFL. There was a pattern there with baseball, with two leagues. There was a void there.

All we really wanted to do was copy a successful format. Unless we made real bad business decisions, we really should have been able to make it succeed. We were lucky in the choice of people. The way some of them came about is just amazing.

Ralph Wilson wrote me a letter in the mail. I kid him about being a mail order franchise. He just wrote a letter. He had heard about the league. He was a minority stock holder in the Lions; he'd be interested in a team in Miami.

Today, he is still 100 percent owner. Bud Adams, Ralph Wilson, Lamar Hunt. We had an ownership continuity that lasted a long, long time. Up until about five years ago, there was an ownership tie with every original team except one, the Titans.

> How do you keep the Raiders out of your front yard?
>
> Paint a goal line across it.

There were minor ownership changes. A team like Oakland had eight or nine partners the first year, and there was some shake out the next. Ed McGah, Baron Hilton. Phipps sold out four years ago, five years ago in Denver. New England, Bill Sullivan headed the original group of 10 people at 10-percent each. Except for two years, when he was forced out and then he came back and bought the other people out. New York made a complete change, but even there they have had the same ownership for 22 years. We have had a lot of continuity, even more so than the average old, NFL teams.

That continuity helped. The financial continuity helped. We had three 100-percent owners. We are all actively involved in the player recruiting process. I don't think you see that today in sports; it is much more complicated today. Bud Adams really worked at player recruiting – that is something he loved.

He didn't mind that it might cost a few more dollars. It meant keeping another player away from the NFL.

I know I didn't have one single thing on paper. I didn't have a typed proposal, or demographics, television markets. I thought demographics was a Yugoslav basketball player.

I told these people (the other eventual AFL owners) I had been to see the Cardinals, that I wanted to see a team in Dallas. It occurred to me that another league might make a go of it. I heard you were interested in the Cardinals.

The NFL is not going to expand, and maybe a second league would be of interest. The conversation was basically very simple. They were pretty short conversations, a couple of hours. Bud Adams took me to dinner. There really wasn't any sales pitch. The numbers were very reasonable. We weren't looking for six million.

We were asking each team to put up $25,000. That would be the league treasury. We were naive to think that would last very long. There were no premonitions in it. It was ready to happen. I think we were lucky to find people who were good football fans and could financially make a commitment. Only exception was Bob Howsam. He was a baseball man. Denver was a city that I happened to believe had great potential. He owned the stadium there for his minor league baseball team. His era lasted just a year. Continuity with minor partners.

Another exception was Harry Wismer, who was under-financed. He was a stock holder in two NFL teams before the AFL. He owned 25 percent of the Redskins and he owned four percent of the Lions in a trust. We required him to sell out to go into the AFL venture. Staying together, and keeping enough financial stability that all survived. There were not wholesale dropouts that happened in other leagues.

We nationalized – that's the wrong word – we *helped* make the game national. It was basically a northern game before. One thing I put on paper. Have you ever seen my map of America? You can take a map of the state of Texas, and lay it over the top of all 10 of these cities. It showed that the game could go national. Instead of the game being concentrated in the northeast, the AFL overnight took it to Denver, Dallas, Houston and Minneapolis. Whole parts of the country with enormous populations did not have pro football.

The AFL really triggered that. It would not have happened nearly that fast without the AFL. It was a snail's pace, sort of like it is now. That was a minor accomplishment. It wasn't the goal we set out with. My interest was seeing Dallas get a team, the Dallas-Houston tie and so on.

One of the most significant things was Sonny Werblin's purchase of the New York Titans. That took our very weakest links and almost overnight, they became one of the strongest ownership groups in the most important media market in the country. Instead of our being the laughingstock there, almost immediately we were on the upper hand, because Sonny had such great manner and image with the media. Just a year later, Shea Stadium was completed. By the second year at Shea, they were selling out. It was a very rapid turnaround.

I personally favored the league moving the team out of New York. We had a chance to sell to somebody in Miami, and I didn't think it was worth staying in New York, playing at the Polo Grounds in front of 5,000 people. I was very short-sighted. I didn't know how strong a guy Sonny could be. Sonny was the guy who got us our second television contract, and that would have to be another very, very important moment, the five-year deal we signed with NBC in February of 1964. My wife Norma and I were on our honeymoon in Innsbruck at the Olympics.

Ralph Wilson was there and more in touch with what was happening. Sonny through his friendships, he succeeded in making us equal to the NFL in monetary standpoint. We only had eight teams. You can imagine if that happened today and somebody came forward and paid the USFL equal money to what we are getting, they would have it made. That was a key.

The good fortune was with the original ownership group. I had no idea how lucky this was, but we didn't end up with a lot of fractionalized ownership. New England had 10 people with 10 percent each. Every new league seems to have that kind of problem. Joe Namath, the great player he was, he was really a public relations creation of Werblin. If you remember that year, he signed two quarterbacks – Namath and John Huarte, who won the Heisman Trophy. He signed them the same season. Namath had the arm, too. They had 41,000 paid the year before Namath played in their first year at Shea Stadium. Second year, they

How do you break a Dolphins fan's finger?

Punch him in the nose.

averaged 58,000, which was essentially capacity. PR wise, the public saw that as one of the very key things.

Only thing I had against Sonny, he wanted us to leave Kansas City. In 1965-66, he wanted us to get out of Denver and KC, and get into Philadelphia and Chicago. Early on, there were stars like Billy Cannon. I think Keith Lincoln was great. He had a great championship game performance. Ernie Ladd was another great player for the Chargers. Kansas City players through the late 1970s were the best. It was ironic. Hard to look back on it now and say, the AFL did not develop its own quarterbacks right away. The people who came into our league and did well were George Blanda, Len Dawson. Namath was one of the first rookie players that came out of college and did well in the AFL. And John Hadl did. We developed a lot of good players early out of college because we had the ability and aggressiveness to sign players to not too big a financial commitment. Our first year we signed Jack Spikes, and I think we gave him $1,000 more than Pittsburgh was offering.

I think it is a lot different situation now. I think we hit a market where it was ready to happen, when the map was ready to expand. There are cities now that would like pro football. There are a bunch of them, Memphis, Birmingham. Those cities are the minority, and are least important in their picture.

They've got to succeed in the big television markets, because they are a television league. We didn't have to succeed in the big markets. Except we felt we wanted a team in New York and Los Angeles 25 years ago, that was part of the verbal train of thought. The difference now is that they had a lot better stadium situation than we did. We couldn't get into Miami because the city of Miami wouldn't rent the Orange Bowl to a pro team. We couldn't go into Seattle. We had a guy who wanted to have an original team, but we couldn't get the University of Washington Stadium. We couldn't get Tulane Stadium in New Orleans. Today, they can get just about any stadium they want. And there are more stadiums around today.

Almost as soon as he signed with the AFL, a player was maligned, and asked, "Why did you do something dumb like that?" People don't seem to ask that question today. In those days, the party line was so hammered out by the NFL that this was an inferior league and so on, there was almost a battle that developed ideologically between old NFL cities. They didn't even report the scores.

Togetherness would be in my top five (reasons the AFL succeeded). We helped each other in recruiting. I can remember making phone calls on behalf of Oakland, trying to get them players, if you can believe that. Lance Alworth, I made a pitch for him. He signed with the Chargers, signed with the league; it was to our own benefit. It was almost unthinkable for a player to jump leagues. Willard Duvall did and after that happened we established a policy that we weren't interested in signing any NFL veterans. As opposed to now, when the first thing you do is go out and raid somebody.

I can't tell you how much we didn't want to buy the Cowboys. Taking it national, the two leagues heightened the interest in both leagues, created the Super Bowl, the

No. 1 event in America today. If the NFL had expanded on a normal schedule of two teams every four or five years, I don't know how many teams they would have. They would still be playing an east and west championship. There never would have been a Super Bowl created. It is hard to believe anything as archaic as that.

It was a pretty big business then, too. It was darn important to me. I had a lot of money in it, a lot invested in it. Emotionally it was something I spent a lot of time and effort and energy on. I felt the obligation. For Bill Sullivan, he had everything he had in it. When we started, NFL teams were thought to be worth $1 million or $2 million. Bud Adams has been quoted as saying he put $1 million in the bank to purchase the Cardinals and he lost about $2 million after about five years.

My, how things have changed.

# How Lamar Hunt Brokered the Biggest Merger in Pro Sports History

*When Lamar Hunt founded the American Football League, the last thing the young Texan dreamed of was joining forces with the more formidable National Football League. Yet, just 10 years after "The Foolish Club's" members proved they weren't so foolish, Hunt took part in a merger that was part cloak and dagger and part dime-novel mystery. The founder tells the story in his own words:*

The first meeting was right out of one of those Scotland Yard spy movies. Tex Schramm of the Dallas Cowboys and I met for the first time in a parking lot at Love Field in Dallas to talk about the possible merger of our American Football League and their NFL. I had been in Kansas City for a Chiefs function that day. Tex called me and asked if it would be possible to get together in the next few days. I was on my way to Houston from Kansas City, so we agreed to meet at Love Field – at the Texas Ranger statue in the lobby at Love Field – to be exact. I said I would get off the plane and we could visit before it took off again for Houston.

I saw him at the statue, waiting, and from there we went to the parking lot and sat in his car and talked for 30 minutes in the dark. Can you imagine if there had been a security guard watching all of this – two strange men in a parked car in the airport parking lot!

We wouldn't have had a chance. Anyway, that was the beginning of the merger discussions. Just Tex and I at first because there were strong feelings on both sides.

Now it's all those years since the merger and, even though I still think of it as the AFL and the NFL, it really isn't anymore. It just doesn't seem like that long because the memories are still vivid in my mind.

**I'm glad we merged. But I will always think of it as the AFL vs. the NFL.**

Over the next month, from those first days in April, Tex and I met face-to-face on two occasions and there were a lot of phone conversations in between. Not too many people knew we were talking because we thought that would be best. We first started talking about how the merger might be attained, finding some common grounds of agreement. Just for Tex and I and then thinking about what would be accepted by others in both leagues.

We knew each other because we both lived in Dallas and we also "fought" each other in Dallas when the Texans and Cowboys were there together from 1960 through 1962. We had already challenged each other to the full extent on the battle field with the Dallas fans and we knew that neither of us would emerge victorious financially or any other way, so we elected to take the AFL Texans north to Kansas City in 1963.

In 1966, there were 111 common draft choices by the two leagues. The NFL signed 79 and the AFL signed 28. Four never signed with either league.

From just a long-range standpoint, the AFL's contract with NBC-TV – a five-year agreement – was the biggest single factor in bringing the two leagues together. It was the most dramatic single development in regard to impact. The Jets established the fact that two teams could do well in New York.

Our Texans left Dallas to the Cowboys, the Chargers left Los Angeles to the Rams and moved to San Diego, but Joe Namath and the Jets were challenging the Giants in New York and the Raiders had a big following in the Bay Area competing against the 49ers.

Yet, when I look back on those times, the biggest stumbling block was the personal antagonism that had gone on for seven years between the two leagues. There was a lot of distrust. I can remember once we got our committee together – Ralph Wilson of the Bills and Billy Sullivan of the Patriots. Both were original AFL owners. They were telling me that the NFL people were just leading me on. I can remember Ralph and Billy were at my home one evening and I got Tex on the phone, just so they could hear it themselves. I still have the paper with Ralph Wilson's handwriting, telling me to ask Tex certain questions as we were going through the conversation.

The negotiations almost ended when the Giants signed Pete Gogolak away from Buffalo. That started the signing war. We, that is the AFL, went after quarterbacks. Houston signed John Brodie to a future contract and there were others along the way, though Brodie's signing got the NFL's attention.

Tex and I, and probably everyone else, knew this couldn't go on. Memorial Day, 1966, was the turning point. I was at the Indianapolis 500, but much of the weekend was spent on the telephone with Schramm, NFL commissioner Pete Rozelle and our AFL committee. Tex and Pete were in Dallas.

The final terms were ironed out:

- One commissioner: Rozelle
- A championship game between the two leagues starting in 1966.
- Inter-league play beginning in the preseason of 1967.
- A common schedule in 1970.

As I look back now, it represented an incredible struggle for survival from our standpoint. It wasn't a matter of if the NFL was going to survive. We were fighting for survival. We were fighting to establish something. We had copied a successful idea.

It was a remarkable era in sports because the American Football League was the first league that had really lasted. There had been three previous American Football Leagues and they had all failed.

Although the American Football League merged into the National name and changed the name to "conference," we still came as a unit and I feel proud of that because there was a lot of pride in the AFL. I think the feeling was that we had succeeded. We had kept the bill collectors away from the door long enough, the wolves away from the door and did succeed from the standpoint of making it a viable entity.

I'm glad we merged. But I will always think of it as the AFL vs. the NFL. I still keep track and always will.

# A Genius, an Innovator and a Hall of Fame Individual

The late Lamar Hunt, the always-smiling, bespectacled founder of the American Football League, certainly doesn't look like he belongs on a dais with the likes of Lance Alworth, Joe Namath, or the Pro Football Hall of Fame members of his beloved Kansas City Chiefs.

"No one deserves to be in the Pro Football Hall of Fame more than Mr. Hunt," said Bobby Bell, the revolutionary outside linebacker who was the first Chiefs player inducted into the pro shrine.

Hall of Fame quarterback Len Dawson agrees.

"I was just sitting around one day, thinking about Lamar and it hit me how many lives the man touched," Dawson said. "Take my case, for example. I wasn't wanted in Cleveland or Pittsburgh and if Lamar hadn't founded the AFL and given guys like me a place to play, who knows what might have happened?

"He's not only a Hall of Famer as a football mastermind, he's a Hall of Famer as an individual."

When he became the first member of the AFL to be enshrined in the Hall of Fame, Hunt could have used his soap box to thumb his nose at those folks who called his venture "The Foolish Club."

But that wasn't the style of the former third-string wide receiver from Southern Methodist University.

"I'm the last person to claim personal justification," Hunt said. "My selection is symbolic of all the general managers, coaches and players who worked for the growth of the American Football League."

**How about his role as a master secret agent?**

Nothing gave Hunt more pleasure than talking about the AFL, whether it was over the phone from his Dallas office, at home, or in his tasteful suite at Arrowhead Stadium. He had told the stories many times over, but his enthusiastic approach made the listener believe this was the first time his thoughts had been made public.

By his own admission, Hunt didn't fit the role of a Hall of Famer.

"Those guys are a lot bigger than me," he joked.

Well, how about his role as a master secret agent?

So many of the early days of the AFL had a cloak-and-dagger feel, like the time the Chiefs coaxed a youngster from Prairie View A&M to climb out of a hotel window so they could sign him away from the Dallas Cowboys.

"It was a fantastically exciting era," Hunt said, grinning and rubbing his hands together. "From 1960 to 1966 it was the battle over players, like when we had to sneak Otis Taylor out of the window of a motel room. There were lawsuits over Billy Cannon and Jimmy Robinson. There were the big contract offers to Namath and others.

"Otis was a senior out of Prairie View A&M, and the Dallas Cowboys were babysitting him in a motel room to keep him away from the AFL scouts back in 1964.

"But one of our scouts, Lloyd Welles, went into the motel and found a janitor to give a message to Otis. Otis climbed out the window of the motel, got into Lloyd's car, and was on the next flight to Kansas City. We signed him the next day."

Players like Taylor, Dawson, Bell and the late Buck Buchanan made the AFL a legitimate league. And before long, their weekend heroics were televised nationally.

"Television was the big factor," Hunt said, when asked about the growth of the league. "We got an ABC-TV contract the first year. It didn't pay much the first five years, but at least we were on the network.

"One of the key games was the 1962 Championship between the Texans and Oilers. We won the game in six quarters. We had an advantage because there was no other game on television that day and there was bad weather around the country. We had a tremendous audience."

An audience that Hunt could never envision back in the early days of the Chiefs, when 6,200 people were showing up for games.

What do you call a Broncos fan in a 3-piece suit?

The defendant.

When asked about his early days at Municipal Stadium, Bob Johnson, the Kansas City horseman who rode the Chiefs mascot, War Paint, said, "You could have shot a shotgun into the stands and no one would have gotten hurt because there weren't any people in the stands.

"But Mr. Hunt believed, and he built a great team, and look at 'em today – 80,000 a game."

Hunt certainly never thought the new league would take off in such dramatic fashion.

"No way," Hunt said. "We couldn't conceptualize what has happened, especially with television. No one believed the numbers would be as high as they are. Not to steal baseball's title, but we have become the national pasttime. People build their schedules around Monday Night Football. It's silly to say we knew it would become this big."

It's hard to believe that Hunt was once a 26-year-old kid whose father was the richest man in America.

Hunt's father was H.L. Hunt, who had an income of more than $1 million per week when he ruled the oil game in Texas. The elder Hunt was not a fan of professional sports endeavors, but the old man had a sense of humor.

When someone told him that Lamar's Dallas Texans lost $1 million, he quipped, "At that rate, they will last only 100 years!"

Just 10 years after the birth of his new league, the AFL merged with the more established NFL and today football has replaced baseball as America's game.

We have the founder of "The Foolish Club" to thank for that.

*Post Script: In August of 2009, the Pro Football Hall of Fame formally opened the Lamar Hunt Super Bowl Gallery in its facility in Canton, Ohio. The special gallery is dedicated entirely to the game's annual showcase – the Super Bowl.*

# Reflections on a 'Great, Great, Great, Great Man' – Lamar Hunt

*"He was a great, great, great, great man. He was just an unbelievable human being – kind, warm, considerate, no ego problems. I had a great relationship with him. I strive to be the same kind of man that he was. He touched my life. He really did. He wanted people to love sports like he did. He loved sports so much, he was so passionate about them and he wanted others to share the joy."*

**- Dick Vermeil, former head coach, Kansas City Chiefs**

*"He saw things and understood things that would be good for the game many, many years ahead of other people."*

**- Norma Hunt, wife**

*"He was a visionary, he was clever, he was creative, he was stubborn, he was optimistic, he was stubbornly optimistic, he looked at things for the long haul."*

**- Clark Hunt, son, and current Chiefs owner**

*"When you talk about humility, Lamar Hunt's name should be in the dictionary under that term because of how he carried himself and how he always put others and thought about others before himself."*

**- Herm Edwards, former head coach, Kansas City Chiefs**

*"Lamar Hunt's a pioneer and a pillar of the National Football League. He's been innovative and creative throughout all the years he's been involved. There aren't enough words to accurately describe who Lamar Hunt was and what he has meant to the NFL and to Kansas City. For the Chiefs, he was our founder. He's the guy who made the decision to move the franchise from Dallas to Kansas City. It was a great decision. To Kansas City, he's more than just the owner of a professional franchise. He's committed himself there with other businesses such as Hunt Midwest Enterprises, creating thousands of jobs throughout the Kansas City community. He's been one of the most philanthropic people I've ever been involved with."*

**- Carl Peterson, former President/GM/CEO, Kansas City Chiefs**

*"All the times that Lamar and I were together in 47 years there was never one day that I felt that I was working for Lamar. He always made me feel I was working with him."*

**- Jack Steadman, retired vice chairman of the board, Kansas City Chiefs**

*"Lamar played the largest role of anyone in football over the course of the last 40 to 50 years. He brought pro football to 10 new cities with the AFL, which was his creation. His place in pro football history is secure. As a person, he was extraordinarily modest and unfailingly pleasant. Everyone – whether a commissioner, owner, player or fan – liked and admired him."*

**- Mike Brown, president, Cincinnati Bengals**

*"Lamar Hunt was one of the greatest leaders and innovators in the history of sports. His vision transformed pro football and helped turn a regional sport into a national passion. Lamar created a model franchise in the Kansas City Chiefs, but he was always equally devoted to the best interests of the league and the game, from the AFL-NFL merger to the two-point conversion. His legacy is unmatched in sports and the NFL – a pioneer, a founding father, and one of the most important architects in the history of our game."*

**- Roger Goodell, NFL Commissioner**

*"He was one of the most considerate, one of the most thoughtful and one of the most visionary people you could ever deal with. Lamar Hunt was a founding father of modern professional sports and a tremendous sports visionary and leader. I first met Lamar in 1969 and had the privilege of working closely with him on an extraordinary range of projects in a number of sports. He always led with vision, tenacity and humility. He played football at Southern Methodist University and was passionate about the game and a perfectionist, as well. Above all else, he was intensely focused on the best interests of the fans – especially his beloved Chiefs fans – and on the collective interests of the league and of his fellow owners, no matter the sport. Norma and Lamar have always been among the most supportive friends and colleagues that Chan and I have had during our decades in the NFL. We will miss Lamar very deeply."*

**- Paul Tagliabue, NFL Commissioner from 1989-2006**

*"When you walked in a room and you saw him and saw he was a part of something, you knew it was something that was branded with integrity and solid and something you could stand behind."*

**- Robert Kraft, owner, New England Patriots**

*"Lamar Hunt had a dream and, the thing is, we had dreams, too. Just imagine the number of people that he has touched because he said, 'I'm going after this dream.'"*

**- Hall of Fame QB Len Dawson**

*"Lamar Hunt went to the NFL and he said, 'I want to buy an NFL team,' or 'I want to put up money to create a team,' and they said, 'No.' That just tickles me to death. (Lamar) said, 'Well, if you don't want to give me a team, I'll just go start my own league.'"*

**- Hall of Fame WR Don Maynard**

*"Lamar Hunt was one of the finest owners in the history of professional football and one of America's greatest sportsmen. It has been my privilege to work with and compete against Lamar. It was an honor for me to have a close relationship with Lamar and with his family, and that came out of 23 years of working together and competing against each other. In my early years, Lamar had a significant influence on me as a new owner in the league."*

**- Pat Bowlen, owner, Denver Broncos**

*"He was someone that you were just attracted to, you wanted to be part of his circle. People just gravitated to him. He had this ability to influence and to turn a room and to communicate his side so effectively with a quiet confidence that was unnerving.*

*He was the man who invented the American Football League and coined the term Super Bowl, but when Lamar was talking about soccer there was that glint in his eye. It's just something very special and when the books are written, the book on American soccer is going to have chapters on Lamar Hunt and what he did both in the past and the present for the game here (in the U.S.)."*

**- Don Garber, Major League Soccer Commissioner**

*"He was so instrumental in making tennis what it is today. He just knew the game hadn't been tapped in bringing sponsors in and creating it as a business and not just a game."*

**- Rod Laver, Grand Slam tennis champion**

*"If Lamar had done for sports in Great Britain what he has done for them here he would have been knighted by the queen."*

**- Kenny Cooper, Dallas Tornados goalie, North American Soccer League**

*"You sort of had this picture of this extremely wealthy Texan who was going to come on big and strong and be really overbearing, but Lamar was just exactly the opposite."*

**- John Newcombe, World Championship Tennis player**

*"I think people need to be aware of what he brought to the sport of tennis: the passion he brought, the love of the game. He was someone who really gave these players an opportunity to go out and make a great living. He cared about the sport. I was lucky that I came at the time where it was just starting to explode and there were a lot of great personalities in the sport. Yet, at the same time, you had at least a sense of appreciation for what a man like Lamar Hunt was laying on the line. What he did was what he continued to do in soccer, which was trying to raise the profile of the sport that is huge worldwide but not as big in the states."*

**- John McEnroe, tennis champion**

*"Lamar was so much more than a contributor to sports. He was a founder and a creator. His vision and his passion shaped the sporting landscape of this country like few others have before him. His innovative drive was inspired by his love of the games, the athletes and the spirit of competition. He was a gentleman. He moved comfortably among the giants of sports and always had the common touch."*

**- Jerry Jones, owner, Dallas Cowboys**

*"I have much admiration for his love of professional football and, of course, the American Football League, which he started. We were rivals, we were friends, we were competitors. Lamar Hunt is a legend and will be sorely missed as he has been a part of our lives for the past five decades."*

**- Al Davis, owner, Oakland Raiders**

*"Lamar has been a good friend, a valued friend since I was fortunate enough to become a part of the league in 1980. He was a good man. Boy, he loved his Chiefs, but just as much, he loved football. He was very modest and soft-spoken, but he was a competitor and wanted to win as much as anyone. And he was always the first man to call whenever congratulations were deserved, even if our team had beaten his team. His word and a handshake was all you ever needed from Lamar."*

**- Alex G. Spanos, owner, San Diego Chargers**

*"The San Diego Chargers exist today, in large part, due to the courage and vision of Lamar Hunt. He was one of the founding fathers of the old American Football League. He, along with the other original AFL owners, had the foresight of what football could become in America and dared to begin a new league in competition against the National Football League. The success of the old AFL caused the merger of the two leagues and has given us the NFL we have today. And after that and throughout his ownership, Lamar was always one of the league's most respected owners and leaders. On countless occasions he was a voice of reason that always helped the league reach the right decision to the betterment of everyone and the future of the game. Everyone who has ever enjoyed the fruits of this great game and league – owner, coach, player alike – owes Lamar Hunt a debt of gratitude today."*

**- Dean Spanos, president, San Diego Chargers**

*"He had an undeniable way to get things done the right way. There was nobody like him. Lamar is the most unique person I have ever known. He led in a quiet but confident way. He was able to build consensus through discussion, and his ultimate objective was to do what was best for the NFL. His demeanor never changed after victory or defeat. He was always interested in what he might do 'to help.' I consider myself most fortunate to have had the privilege to know and work with Lamar. His contributions to the National Football League as we know it today are unparalleled, and his presence and friendship will be missed."*

**- Marty Schottenheimer, former head coach, Kansas City Chiefs**

*"Among the role models that I observed both up-close and from a distance was Mr. Hunt. Over many decades he, in my opinion, stayed firm in his views and yet was gracious and easygoing. Nobody can invent and achieve on Lamar Hunt's level without enormous intelligence and passion and yet very few of those do so with such an enduring niceness and restraint."*

**- Randy Lerner, owner, Cleveland Browns**

*"He was truly a gentleman, a smart guy and very respectful. I think he respected the game a lot, too. When he spoke in league meetings, you always had the sense that he was speaking from the heart, what was best for the game. It wasn't about what was best for the Chiefs. It was about what was best for the game and I think that came across in a genuine, sincere manner, so I believed it."*

**- Bill Belichick, head coach, New England Patriots**

*"Lamar Hunt's immense wisdom and creative genius drew strength from a child's inquisitive mind and gentle heart. He embodied the fearless vision to create, but also the unselfish caretaker's touch to nurture, like a spiritual gardener in tune with nature's four seasons. The American sports fan, and specifically all NFL fans, should know that Lamar Hunt fearlessly represented their interests and their investment in our great game like no other. We will never see the likes of this gentle giant in the National Football League again."*

**- Jim Irsay, owner, Indianapolis Colts**

*"Lamar Hunt was one of the giants of sports in America and the NFL, in particular. A chronicle of his contributions could fill two books. His counsel was wise and always in the best interests of the game and the league. He was a leader in the truest sense of the word. He was a gentleman in the truest sense of the word."*

**- Bill Polian, president, Indianapolis Colts**

*"In every way, Mr. Hunt stood for all the best values and principles. He was a giant of industry, a visionary and consummate sportsman, but he was even greater as a person and family man. I am most fortunate for having worked for Mr. Hunt. The seasons I spent with him have provided special memories I will carry always."*

**- Tony Dungy, former assistant coach, Kansas City Chiefs, and former head coach, Indianapolis Colts**

*"On a professional level, he was a leader of men and he was instrumental in transforming the game of football into what it is today. We owe him a debt of gratitude on his vision and leadership. Our league has lost a great man, but in that, we are all beneficiaries of his tremendous vision."*

**- Tom Benson, owner, New Orleans Saints**

*"He was not one to flaunt it, he just did it . . . I knew Lamar for close to 50 years. He was a friend, a business associate, a family man, a visionary – one of the finest men I have ever known. We shared a love of sports and the dream of football ownership that became a reality in 1960. He will always be remembered by me and others as one of the greats."*

**- K.S. "Bud" Adams, Jr., founder and owner, Tennessee Titans**

*"His humility and caring ways stand out. He made the NFL better with his suggestions regarding improving the game, and he always put the fans first."*

**- Art Modell, minority owner, Baltimore Ravens**

*"Everyone talks about Lamar Hunt as a founder, a pioneer and as a sportsman, and he certainly was all of those things. But I will remember him more as a man of integrity and decency. He was a great example of how owners of professional sports franchises should conduct themselves."*

**- John Mara, president/CEO, New York Giants**

*"The National Football League is indebted to Lamar Hunt for his vision and foresight and his incredible understanding of how great our sport and our league could become. And he exerted his influence with tremendous humility and passion."*

**- Steve Tisch, chairman/executive vice president,
New York Giants**

*"Lamar Hunt was one of the outstanding visionaries in modern sports. He was a leader in our ownership group and spent more than 40 years to help make pro football America's passion. Whether it was his role in helping start the old AFL from scratch, his leadership in helping forge the merger between the two leagues, or his role in developing the Super Bowl into the preeminent single event in American sports, he played an instrumental role in making the NFL the most successful sports league in the world. Besides being a tremendous owner, though, he first and foremost was a fan. He cared deeply about the Chiefs and about the game of football, and was one of the biggest assets the NFL has ever had."*

**- H. Wayne Huizenga, owner, Miami Dolphins**

*"Lamar Hunt was one of the great sportsmen in our country. His contribution to the success of the NFL and sports has been extraordinary. What I will always cherish about Lamar was his decency, humility and his intelligent and soft-spoken manner."*

**- Jeffrey Lurie, chairman/CEO, Philadelphia Eagles**

*"He graciously shared his thoughts and wisdom with me from the first day I became the owner of an NFL team. His vision and guidance helped keep the NFL on track."*

**- Daniel Snyder, owner, Washington Redskins**

*"Lamar Hunt's creative foresight impacted the National Football League throughout his involvement with the Kansas City Chiefs and the league. His contribution to professional football and other sports has left an indelible mark."*

**- Joel Glazer, executive vice president, Tampa Bay Buccaneers**

*"Without Lamar Hunt, the National Football League would not be as we know it today. He had a vision that has exceeded anyone's expectations, and the fans, players and coaches as well as NFL owners are the benefactors of this vision. He put the league's interests above his own and everyone who loves pro football will always be indebted to him."*

**- Jerry Richardson, owner, Carolina Panthers**

*"Lamar Hunt was one of the most highly regarded owners in the NFL. His integrity was beyond reproach and his intellect was a great asset to the NFL. He built a small city franchise into a powerhouse by broadening his fan base to the multi-state region surrounding Kansas City. His success in running a franchise is a model for all of us. Lamar was a friend to all of us and out of respect for him, I called on him when selecting a name for our new Houston team since his team was originally the Dallas Texans. I asked if he would mind if I selected the Texans name for our team, and he*

*responded with delight that he would be honored if we did."*

**- Bob McNair, owner, Houston Texans**

*"Lamar Hunt was a pioneer that was willing to sacrifice for the good of the league. We have all benefited from his vision and contributions to the NFL and the sports world."*

**- NFL Hall of Fame coach Joe Gibbs**

*"Lamar has to be considered one of the giants of the game. He probably did more than anyone else to get the two leagues (the AFL and the NFL) together, and that led to pro football becoming America's number one sport. Some of my greatest memories are games we played against his teams. The playoff contest on Christmas Day in 1971 remains one of the greatest games in NFL history and one of the greatest wins I've ever been associated with. We actually closed his old stadium that day and opened his new one the next year, which was the first game of our undefeated season. Because he was such a passionate fan and cared so much about the sport, I always enjoyed competing against his teams, and he did as much as anyone to make the NFL the great league it is today."*

**- NFL Hall of Fame coach Don Shula**

*"Lamar Hunt was a great pioneer of professional football. His impact on the National Football League was tremendous. I really admired the way the NFL was most important to him – he always thought that what was best for the league was best for all 32 teams. He also had a great feel for Green Bay. He brought some friends from Dallas to Lambeau Field for a Packers-Chiefs game and they walked through the parking lot, visited with tailgaters and then took in the game. Afterward, he wrote to tell me what a marvelous place this is and how proud he was to be in the same league with the Green Bay Packers. That is quite a memory for me."*

**- Bob Harlan, chairman/CEO, Green Bay Packers**


*"Lamar Hunt was a great man in many respects. He was one of the founding fathers of professional football, a tremendous innovator, and a superb businessman who possessed great integrity. His strong work ethic and vision helped transform the NFL from a regional attraction to a national passion, and his strong knowledge of the inner-workings of professional football allowed the Kansas City Chiefs to become one of the NFL's model franchises. Lamar embodied so many special qualities. He was a man of great substance who had a sense of humility and caring for all people. He was truly unique."*

**- Arthur Blank, owner, Atlanta Falcons**

*"Lamar's contributions to professional football and to the sports world are well documented. He was also a very generous and civic minded individual and a steadfast supporter of the Pro Football Hall of Fame, and he had been a member of the Board of Trustees since 1968."*

**- Steve Perry, president, Pro Football Hall of Fame**

# The Legendary Chiefs

Many great players have worn the uniform of the Kansas City Chiefs. But only a handful have become Pro Football Hall of Famers.

This section is about those Legendary Chiefs.

*"He could do it all. He could throw a football the length of the playing field, outrun most halfbacks, and punt with the best of 'em. He was our long snapper and a standout on special teams."*

# The Greatest Outside Linebacker (and Practical Joker) in Chiefs History

It should come as no surprise to any Kansas City Chiefs fan that Bobby Bell was the first player from the team's glory years to be inducted into the Pro Football Hall of Fame.

"Bobby could have played any position on the field – including quarterback," said Hall of Fame quarterback and former teammate Len Dawson. "He could punt, he was our long snapper, he played on kickoff and punt return teams and he was the best linebacker in the history of the AFL."

While team founder Lamar Hunt was the first member of the Chiefs family to be inducted into the Hall, Bell was the first player.

"I never thought I was good enough to make it," Bell said. "I was so surprised when I found out. It was the greatest honor of my life."

And who did he pick as his presenter?

"Coach (Hank) Stram," he said, smiling. "Who else would I pick?"

Because Bell was a star on the field, the eight-time AFL and NFL Pro Bowl linebacker could get away with some pretty unique practical jokes at practice.

And most of the time, the jokes were aimed at Stram, the fiery head coach.

"Coach liked to watch practice from this cherry picker," Bell said, laughing at the memory. "He was a short guy and he could see the entire practice field from up there. He'd be yelling at us, and getting on our nerves, so one day he goes up in the picker and I take the distributor cap so it can't come back down."

In a move that was highly unusual for Stram, he congratulated the team on a great practice and said over his loud speaker, "No running today boys! Great practice!"

Bell was wondering what was going on, and he found out as he walked to the locker room.

"They had (groundskeeper) George Toma out there with this long ladder and Hank was climbing down from the cherry picker," Bell said. "I was laughing so hard I was crying."

The next day, when Bell and his teammates arrived at practice, the cherry picker's inner workings were protected by a couple of padlocks.

"He told me it was my butt if I ever did it again," Bell said, "but that was just the relationship we had. I loved to play practical jokes on him, but I loved playing for him even more."

While Stram enjoyed the antics on the practice field, he really

> ££ Coach liked to watch practice from this cherry picker. He was a short guy and he could see the entire practice field from up there. He'd be yelling at us, and getting on our nerves, so one day he goes up in the picker and I take the distributor cap so it can't come back down. JJ
> – Bobby Bell recalling a joke on Hank Stram

treasured those moments when Bell would turn a game around with a great play.

"I don't know if I ever coached a greater athlete than Bobby Bell," Stram said of the outside linebacker who starred in the Chiefs' famous "stack defense."

"He could do it all. He could throw a football the length of the playing field, outrun most halfbacks and punt with the best of 'em. He was our long snapper and a standout on special teams."

Bell was an honor student at the University of Minnesota, where he won the Outland Trophy, given to the top interior lineman in the country. At 6'4", 228 pounds, he was small by defensive end standards, but the Chiefs were depleted at that position in 1963 and they used the seventh pick of the draft to select the future Hall of Famer.

"I didn't know anything about the Chiefs or Kansas City," Bell said. "I know that when Mr. (Lamar) Hunt picked me up at the airport he didn't have enough money to pay the cabbie and I immediately called my (agent) and asked, 'Did I do the right thing by signing with this team?' Looking back on it, I now know I did the right thing."

So did the Chiefs.

"Bobby was amazing," Dawson said. "They talk about Dick Butkus and Ray Nitschke and they were great linebackers – but they weren't any better than Bobby."

# The Chiefs' "Immovable Rock"

Kansas City Chiefs Hall of Fame linebacker Willie Lanier doesn't like to talk about his personal accomplishments all that much.

Oh, he'll be happy to tell you about his two AFL All-Star starts, six NFL Pro Bowl appearances, a Hall of Fame ring, and being named to the NFL's 75th Anniversary All-Time Team.

But he would be delighted to talk for hours about his love of the Chiefs and the fact that he was part of something special in Kansas City.

"It was wonderful playing for (coach) Hank Stram because of his winning record and his positive attitude," Lanier said. "He put together the best group of players that could compete and show the kind of confidence that he did.

"The benefits of playing – the games won and lost, the championships, the trophies, the yellow press clippings – are all temporary. But the friendships are the things that last forever."

Friendships – and the sound of No. 63 ripping into an opposing running back or tight end.

---

*I once heard someone refer to Willie Lanier as the Black Butkus. That's an insult to Willie Lanier.*

---

Perhaps the greatest compliment Lanier ever received came from another pretty decent linebacker: Dick Butkus, the former Chicago Bears great who is considered to be the standard by which every other linebacker is measured.

When attending a celebrity golf tournament in Kansas City, Butkus was asked about Lanier.

"I once heard someone refer to Willie Lanier as the 'Black Butkus,'" Butkus said. "That's an insult to Willie Lanier. There was never a better linebacker in the NFL."

In a different era, when teams selected players on a hunch, rather than on the advice of a group of computer-analyzing scouts and advance men, Lanier was an unknown commodity at tiny Morgan State University.

"In the 1967 college draft the Chiefs had the good fortune to have two No. 2 draft choices," team founder Lamar Hunt said. "We thought our college scouting was fairly thorough at that time, but the facts are that by today's standards we were back in the stone ages. The Chiefs used both of those No. 2 draft choices at the linebacker position. And we found two players destined to star for 10 years.

"The first one came from a major college power, Notre Dame, where we drafted the captain of their national championship team, Jim Lynch. In the second round, we selected Willie Lanier from a small college in Baltimore called Morgan State University. It is ironic that even though we took Willie in the second round, we had not previously talked to him in person. No member of our organization had really had a conversation with him. Willie had been discovered by a part-time scout named Frank Barnes who was a friend of Hank Stram's who did scouting for us on a regular basis, but he wasn't on our staff.

"To say that Willie was a sleeper was an understatement. But the ultimate decision on draft day was made by Hank. Once Hank saw Jim Lynch and Willie in training camp, he decided that both of them should play and he moved Lynch to the outside and Lanier was to play his middle position as a forceful bear of a man whose strength and intensity and striking power set new standards for the game. In Kansas City, Willie Lanier played on one of the greatest defensive teams in pro football history. He was the immovable rock who had to be avoided at all costs by the offense. In the frozen 1969 playoff game in Shea Stadium, it was his tears and determination that helped stop the Jets on what was the goal line stand, the all-time goal line stand in the Kansas City Chiefs' history."

Yet, it's the people Lanier recalls with such passion. So much so, that when he was inducted into the Hall of Fame, he shared his honor with his former teammates.

"I really don't think back on the wins and losses," Lanier said. "I went to Kansas City and built a lasting relationship with players and coaches of such high quality.

"I know that the rest of the teammates that I played with at Kansas City all share this honor with me and I feel that this is for all of you and for all of us."

It didn't take Lanier long to earn an endearing nickname in Kansas City.

"Oh man, would Willie ever pop people," said Chiefs great Bobby Bell. "There was just this certain sound when he hit someone. It was like 'Ka-whack!' You didn't even need to see the play, you just knew that Willie had done some damage."

The sound made an impression on former Chiefs All-AFL defensive lineman Jerry Mays.

"My first year in Kansas City I followed the style of tackling that we were taught at that time," Lanier said. "You were taught to use your head first and hit players in the middle of their body. It was done in a rather aggressive manner. So, Jerry Mays is the one that I remember that first started calling me 'Contact.'"

Unlike many of his new teammates, Lanier arrived before the start of the 1968 season, and missed the excitement and drama of the first Super Bowl.

"I missed the first Super Bowl by a season," Lanier said, "but I was part of Super Bowl IV and will never forget the feeling after that game. I'm not an emotional person, but the emotions were flowing after we beat the Vikings. It was the last time an AFL club would ever play an NFL club because of the merger and we felt like we were playing for the entire league."

# The Gentle Giant with the Big Heart

There was an important reason the Kansas City Chiefs dominated play in the glory days of the American Football League.

"It all had to do with Lamar Hunt and his willingness to go down South and recruit the top black players in the country," Hall of Fame linebacker Bobby Bell said.

"Look at Big Buck Buchanan. He played at Grambling, and back then, teams didn't pay much attention to schools like Grambling, or Morgan State – which produced a pretty good linebacker named Willie Lanier.

"Mr. Hunt wanted to build a championship team, and he went about it the right way. When he drafted Buck Buchanan he got a guy who anchored the defensive line for a decade – a true Hall of Famer."

When the Chiefs defeated the Minnesota Vikings in Super Bowl IV, Buchanan called it his greatest football thrill.

In his many speaking engagements around the Kansas City area, he would take off his huge Super Bowl ring and slip it on the finger of an awe-struck fan.

"I wanted to share everything we did with the fans," Buchanan said.

Perhaps the only thing that surpassed the feeling he experienced following Super Bowl IV came when he was enshrined in the Pro Football Hall of Fame in 1990.

"That was incredible," he said.

By the time of the induction ceremony, Buchanan had begun chemotherapy treatment in his battle against cancer.

With his body weakened by the disease, he accepted his Hall of Fame ring before a sold-out crowd at Arrowhead Stadium as fellow Chiefs Hall of Famers and former teammates applauded and wiped away tears.

"That was a tough day," Hall of Fame quarterback Len Dawson said. "We knew then that Buck wasn't going to be with us for much longer. And we all loved him. He was just a special player, but an even more special man."

In typical Buchanan fashion, after he accepted his ring, Buchanan told the cheering fans, "This belongs to Kansas City."

That was his last appearance at Arrowhead Stadium. He died on July 16, 1992, at the age of 51.

Buchanan's wife, Georgia, who is still active in the community and represents her husband at the annual Chiefs reunion game, still remembers the love that team owner Lamar Hunt and his wife, Norma, showed following Buck's death.

"Lamar was on his way to Dallas," Georgia said, "and when he heard about Buck's death he came to our home for three days. He answered the phone, answered the door, made sure Buck's funeral plans were followed. I'll never forget what he did for our family. He was there when we really needed him."

And Buchanan was there when the Chiefs needed a defensive stand.

He was the first true giant of the American Football League. By today's standards, his 6'7", 281-pound frame might not be unusual.

"But back then, people looked at Buck and said, 'Wow!'" Bell said.

Buchanan and Bell combined to lead the College All-Stars to a stunning upset of the world champion Green Bay Packers in 1963.

The Dallas Texans, of the upstart American Football League, won a furious bidding war with the NFL and signed Buchanan with the No. 1 pick in the draft. He proved to be a wise choice as he won two team MVP Awards and was a six-time All-AFL player and two-time member of the Pro Bowl.

"I didn't feel that much pressure being drafted No. 1," Buchanan said, "because I had played against some of the best college players in the country and I could hold my own with them.

"There weren't many players as big as I was back in the 1960s and I knew Coach (Hank) Stram was going to make the most of my size and ability. But I kept putting on weight and he was always after me to get into better condition. I played between 286 and 292 pounds.

"I didn't play right away because we had some pretty good defensive linemen – Jerry Mays, Mel Branch, Paul Rochester and Bobby Bell (who went on to become a Hall of Fame linebacker). Bell got hurt about five games into the season and coach put me in at defensive end and I never left."

Buchanan was part of what many believe was the best draft class in team history, as it included future Chiefs Ring of Fame members Ed Budde and Bell.

"You knew that we were going to be good, you could just sense it," Buchanan said. "We moved from Dallas to Kansas City my rookie year and it took a while for us to really become a team. We had some great players, and when we became a team, we became a team of champions."

Buchanan anchored the defense on the 1966 team that won the AFC championship and the right to meet Green Bay in the first Super Bowl.

"That meant a lot to me to play in that game," Buchanan said, "It meant a lot to all the guys. I remember walking down the tunnel to the field before the game. So many people had called us the Mickey Mouse League and had said some pretty bad things about us and here we were, ready to play the Green Bay Packers."

> **" I remembered the NFL players and coaches calling us Mickey Mouse, and now, it didn't matter. We were the champions. "**
>
> *– Buck Buchanan*

Although the Packers claimed a 35-10 victory, Buchanan thought his team could play with the perennial NFL powerhouse.

"Bobby (Bell) and I weren't afraid of them because we'd played on that College All-Star team that beat them in 1963," Buchanan said. "But names like (Vince) Lombardi and (Bart) Starr carried a lot of weight. I don't know – our guys just didn't have a lot of confidence going into that game."

But that all changed three years later when the Chiefs manhandled heavily favored Minnesota 23-7 to win Super Bowl IV.

"We had big defensive games against the Raiders and the Jets to get to the Super Bowl and we were so much bigger than the Vikings we were all relaxed and confident. We were so dominating in the first half, when Jan (Stenerud) kicked the third field goal and we went up 9-0 we felt like they couldn't come back. Then Otis

(Taylor) scores on the long touchdown pass and that was it. It was a great feeling.".

Buchanan's emotions flowed following the game.

"I was so proud when the New York Jets beat Baltimore the year before, because an AFL team had beaten an NFL team in the Super Bowl," Buchanan said. "Now, I'm part of an AFL win in the Super Bowl. I remembered the NFL players and coaches calling us Mickey Mouse, and now, it didn't matter. We were the champions."

# AFL's Most Innovative Coach Finally Gets Call from the Hall of Fame

When Hank Stram and the Kansas City Chiefs came to Municipal Stadium, there were no welcoming parades, glitzy galas or keys to the city.

"Back then, most people just thought of Kansas City as a cow town," Hall of Fame quarterback Len Dawson said. "Then Hank and the Chiefs came to town, and all that changed. People saw Hank and the way he dressed, the confidence he had, and they found out he was a darned good coach, too.

"A lot of things changed in this town, and a lot of it changed because of Hank Stram."

Another Hall of Famer, linebacker Willie Lanier, agrees.

"When you're a part of something as successful as the Chiefs are in Kansas City today, more than 45 years later, that's greatness," Lanier said. "And he was a great, great coach. He was the foundation of what we have today."

In the eyes of Chiefs football fans, Stram will always be remembered for his natty attire, the way he strutted up and down the sidelines, and his byline offensive play, "65 Toss Power Trap."

*Let's matriculate that ball down the field.*

"He was an innovator," Dawson said, "he really was. I don't think that fans really appreciated what Hank meant to Kansas City or the NFL until long after he was gone."

Dawson paused for a moment, smiled and added, "Well, unless they saw our Super Bowl video. Then, they knew what he was all about."

Stram became the first coach to ever wear a microphone during a Super Bowl game, and he became as famous for his wise-cracking remarks such as, "Let's matriculate that ball down the field," as he did for his brilliant play calling.

"We had a 9-0 lead in the third quarter and had the ball on the 4 and needed a score to put the game away," Dawson said. "I'm in the huddle and here comes Gloster Richardson into the game with a play. He says 'Coach wants you to run 65 Toss Power Trap.' I said, 'We haven't run that play in a really long time, are you sure that's what he wants?' Gloster says, 'Yes, it's 65 Toss Power Trap.'"

> ❝ Hank was symbolic of the coaching style and personality of the AFL. Maybe he wouldn't have gotten a chance anywhere else. But he personified the old AFL because he was a salesman. He was an innovator – he wasn't afraid to try new things. ❞
> – *Lamar Hunt on coach Hank Stram*

Stram had spotted something in the Vikings defensive alignment and called perhaps the most famous play in Super Bowl history. Running back Mike Garrett scored a touchdown on the play, giving the Chiefs a commanding 16-0 lead, and Stram walked up and down the sidelines saying to anyone who would listen, "I told you it would work. It was like stealing."

The Chiefs were at the top of their game and Stram was considered the most innovative coach around. But it wasn't always like that for the man who finally got his due respect and was voted into the Pro Football Hall of Fame in 2003.

Stram was a 35-year-old assistant coach at the University of Miami in 1959 when Lamar Hunt hired him as the first head coach of the Dallas Texans. He also had had stops at SMU and Notre Dame – where Stram was part of Terry Brennan's staff that was fired the same day the Stram family received their Christmas cards that said, "CHEER, CHEER FOR OLD NOTRE DAME." The coach was considering a career change.

"I had a family and we were tired of moving all over the country," Stram said. "I was going to be a sporting goods salesman. Then, I got a call that changed my life. It was from Lamar Hunt."

Hunt, an SMU alumnus and former bench-warming wide receiver, had met Stram when he was an assistant coach with the Mustangs.

"I didn't remember meeting Lamar, but when he called, he asked me about my football philosophy, the people we knew in the Dallas area and about this new league he was thinking about forming. He sounded pretty serious, like he really had a plan and was going to do it."

After that football season, Stram attended a banquet at his old high school in Gary, Indiana, and was informed that he had a long-distance phone call. It was from Hunt. He wanted Stram to visit him in Dallas.

"I was at a critical point in my career. I'd said that if I hadn't been offered a head coaching job by a certain age, then I was going to do something else. That sporting goods job was offering me more than I was making at Miami and a lot of coaches got hit with that tag that they're just good enough to be assistants. I didn't want that to happen to me."

For 14 years, he was the only head coach in the history of the Texans and the Chiefs. In the 10-year history of the AFL, Stram's Texans/Chiefs won more games than any other AFL team and more championships than any other coach (1962, 1966, 1969).

He went on to become the only coach in AFL history to take his team to two Super Bowls, losing to the Green Bay Packers in Super Bowl I and defeating the Minnesota Vikings in Super Bowl IV. His 23-7 Super Bowl IV victory over the Vikings gave credibility to the entire AFL, which would merge with the NFL the following season.

"When I met with Lamar, we talked about a philosophy. Lamar was patient and he was willing to do what it took to get the best players and coaches. He let the players play and the coaches coach. He believed that the coach should have supreme authority and make the personnel decisions. You can't run a successful team or program with divided responsibilities. Players are looking for a leader, especially the younger players on a team – and they get that leadership from the coaches and veterans."

Hunt called Stram the face of the AFL.

"Hank was symbolic of the coaching style and personality of the AFL," Hunt said. "Maybe he wouldn't have gotten a chance anywhere else. But he personified the old AFL because he was a salesman. He was an innovator – he wasn't afraid to try new things."

While Hunt made a bold move by making a lifetime assistant his head coach in Dallas, Stram made an even bolder statement by bringing a quarterback to camp that two NFL teams had cast on the scrap heap.

Stram was an assistant when Dawson was an All-America at Purdue. Dawson was a No. 1 draft pick in the NFL, but couldn't gain a starting job in Pittsburgh, where Hall of Famer Bobby Layne was running the offense, or Cleveland, where they had a quarterback named Milt Plum who simply handed the ball off to one of the greatest backs to ever play the game in Jim Brown.

"Len was at the wrong place at the wrong time – twice," Stram said. "My friends would come and watch practice and they would ask me, 'Why did you bring in Dawson? He's washed up.' I told them he was like fine silver and had to have the tarnish removed."

Dawson will forever be grateful to his former coach for not judging him on his first preseason with the Texans.

"I was horrible," Dawson said. "All I did in Pittsburgh was hold for field goals and all I did in Cleveland was sit on the bench and listen to (coach and founder) Paul Brown run down the AFL. Hank was very patient with me. Most coaches would have cut me, and to be honest with you, I've often wondered what would have happened in my life if he would have cut me. I was very fortunate that he was my head coach."

*Why don't the Raiders have a team website?*

*Because they can't string 3 W's together.*

Dawson recalls the game in which he finally felt like he belonged, like he could be a starting quarterback in the AFL and quell all the questions about his ability.

"We were playing the Patriots in the Cotton Bowl before a private showing of fans," quipped Dawson, an intensely private individual who also has a biting sense of humor, "and the game was really tight. There were about as many fans in the seats as there were players on the field, and we have a big third-and-one play. I call a deep pass play and I'll never forget it – I threw a perfect pass, perfect spiral to Bill Miller and he caught it for a first down. A lot of people were questioning Hank about my ability and I think I gained everyone's respect on that play. It was just one of those plays you never forget. You could just sense a whole new confidence from my teammates, and I know Hank was happy."

Stram was soon considered one of the real innovators of the AFL, using a "moving pocket" to exploit the talent of his quarterback, and "stack defense" in which his linebackers would stack behind a defensive lineman. Whether he used a 3-4 defensive alignment or a 4-3, Stram always wanted a defensive player nose to nose with the opposing team's center.

"Team's just didn't do that back then," Dawson said. "I think it's a big reason we won Super Bowl IV, because we had a 290-pound guy (Curly Culp) on their 230-pound center (Mick Tingelhoff)."

While Stram will always be remembered for his offensive brilliance, he took great pride in his defensive schemes.

"The Vikings didn't know what hit 'em in Super Bowl IV," Stram said. "Tingelhoff had never had a guy nose-to-nose with him, especially a guy who weighed 290 pounds. They couldn't run the ball and they had a hard time getting anything going offensively.

"Our offense was very efficient. Lenny did a great job running the offense and we got the big touchdown with 65 Toss Power Trap."

Just mentioning that play brings a grin to the face of the man who won more games than any other AFL coach and re-defined the way the game would be played.

"Coaching the Chiefs was so special," he said. "When we lost the first Super Bowl (35-10 to the Green Bay Packers) it was a professional blow. Our organization didn't lose, the entire league lost. And we felt that and it was tough to deal with. They were calling us the Mickey Mouse League and those comments hurt.

"That's why it was so important to get back to the Super Bowl and represent our league in the last game ever played between an AFL team and an NFL team. When we won, I can't even describe the feeling, the excitement. I remember all the guys in the locker room and how happy they were, and how relieved Lenny was (being named the MVP of the game after having his name linked with a Detroit gambler earlier in the week). In all the bedlam I went over and told him he had a phone call, it was from the President of the United States. Finally it was time to leave and the only two people left in the locker room were me and my good friend Monsignor Vincent Mackey of St. Cecilia's Parish in the Back Bay of Boston. Sitting on a table in the corner was the Super Bowl trophy. Mackey went over and picked it up and we left."

That was Stram's last great moment as coach of the Chiefs. The following year his team missed out on the "dynasty" tag by losing one of the most talked about games in the history of the NFL – the Christmas Day, 27-24 two-overtime playoff loss to Miami in the last game ever played at Kansas City's Municipal Stadium.

For a grueling 82 minutes and 40 seconds, the two best teams in the American Football Conference banged heads, with the Dolphins coming away with a win when Garo Yepremian kicked a 37-yard game-winning field goal.

"It was just a devastating loss," Stram said. "We had been to two of the first four Super Bowls, with one win and one loss. If we would have won that game I think we would have gone on and won another Super Bowl, and who knows how that might have influenced the way people looked at our team. But we had a great run, and I loved every minute of it."

While Stram was known for his "firsts," he achieved another one when he was inducted into the Pro Football Hall of Fame in 2003.

He became the first inductee to have his acceptance speech taped, as his body was so ravaged by the effects of a longtime battle with diabetes he couldn't stand and speak on the podium.

"Can you imagine?" asked Dawson. "As much as Hank liked to talk, if he could have been healthy enough to give his acceptance speech, he might still be up there."

In his taped comments, Stram proved his body might be suffering, but his mind was still as bright and sharp as ever.

"As I matriculate my way down the field of life, I will never forget this moment and you wonderful people who have helped make this day possible."

And anyone who has ever worn a Chiefs jersey or cap, waved a banner or stepped foot in old Municipal Stadium or Arrowhead Stadium over the past 50 years will never forget Hank Stram.

He passed away at the age of 82 in 2005.

# The "Quiet Assassin"

Len Dawson is the seventh son of a seventh son.

"All my life people told me that was good luck," said Dawson, the Kansas City Chiefs Hall of Fame quarterback. "I know one thing. I was fortunate that Lamar Hunt decided to form the American Football League, because all I was doing in the NFL was sitting on the bench and listening to guys bad mouth that 'other league.'"

Dawson, who wasted away for five years in the NFL while trying to crack the starting lineup of the Pittsburgh Steelers and Cleveland Browns, wasn't an immediate pick for the Hall of Fame. But when his time to step into the spotlight happened in 1987, he lived up to his nickname of "Lenny the Cool."

"I remember talking to (Hall of Famer) Bobby Mitchell at the Pro Bowl Game in Hawaii after it was announced that I was going to be inducted and he said, 'Lenny the Cool, I'm going to watch you melt.'"

It didn't happen.

"Some people might call it sweat, but I called it perspiration when I accepted the honor," Dawson said, laughing. "I guess I made it through it all right. I'm still here to talk about it, so it must have been okay.

"You don't make the Hall of Fame by yourself. You need an awful lot of help. I was very fortunate because I was surrounded by very talented people throughout my entire career."

Under his leadership, the Chiefs won three AFL titles and a Super Bowl championship. He earned the nickname "Lenny the Cool" because he never blinked in the oncoming rush of a Ben Davidson or some other form of AFL danger.

If you're lucky enough to be a Chiefs fan, you're lucky enough!

*He never had to open his mouth because he said a lot with his eyes.*

"Lenny was just a remarkable leader and quarterback," Hall of Fame Chiefs coach Hank Stram said. "He was cool, but I called him the quiet assassin. He said a lot with expressions. He never had to open his mouth because he said a lot with his eyes."

When a teammate fouled up, Dawson didn't say a word.

"He didn't need to," said former running back Ed Podolak. "He'd just give you a quick glance and you'd know what he was thinking. We all respected Lenny. He was our leader and he was the Chiefs."

Dawson didn't just earn that respect on the playing field.

"I remember one practice when it was about 105 degrees with 95 percent humidity," he said. "It was so hot, you couldn't breathe. It was like practicing in a sauna. Coach Stram had a thing called the winning edge, which was a series of drills we did before practice even began.

"I mean, they knocked you out."

During one lackluster practice session, Stram stopped practice and demanded that his players go through the winning edge.

"There was a lot of moaning and groaning," Podolak recalls, "and all of a sudden Lenny yells, 'He ain't gonna kill me. I love this!' And he takes off and begins doing the drills. If that's not leadership, I don't know what is."

When asked about the incident, Dawson simply smiled.

"I didn't say much," Dawson said. "I didn't need to. But when I did, the guys took notice. It's a compliment that Ed would remember something like that after all these years."

For most of the Chiefs' 50 years, Dawson has been a part of the team – on the field or in the broadcast booth. He is still an award-winning color commentator for the Chiefs broadcasts, and recently retired as a sports anchor at KMBC-TV 9 in Kansas City.

"Let's see, I joined the Dallas Texans after their second season, they moved to Kansas City in 1963 and I was one of the first pro athletes to take a television job," Dawson said, pausing a moment to recall how many years he'd been at Channel 9. "When we moved to Kansas City from Dallas, they talked to me about being a sports anchor. I thought it sounded interesting, so we would get done with practice at 5:30, I'd shower and get to the studio and do the 6 o'clock newscast. Then I'd go home, have dinner with my family and go back and do the 10 o'clock show. I had someone ask me the other day if there was any place I like to go when I'm not working and I told them, 'I'm always working.'"

He had been a part of the KMBC sports team 45 years and at one time was the lead analyst for NBC sports.

"I enjoy working with the Chiefs," he said. "When I left NBC, I began broadcasting Chiefs games back in 1984 – during the down years. They just weren't very good back then. It was pretty lean until Carl (Peterson) and Marty (Schottenheimer) came in 1989. They turned things around and there was no more exciting place in the NFL than Arrowhead Stadium on a Sunday afternoon.

"I don't know if the fans here realize how highly regarded they are around the league and by our opponents. It's tough to play at Arrowhead because it's so noisy. That sea of red really makes a difference. Just ask our coaches or our players."

Dawson has made his mark in the broadcasting profession for his tell-it-like-I-see-it approach to the game.

"I just tell the listener what I see," he said. "If I see a bad play, I call it a bad play. Then I try to explain what happened. It's almost like watching game film with a player. You go through what happened and analyze it. I really think that the transition from sports to the real world was made easier because of my broadcasting career."

# From Norway to the Hall of Fame

Bobby Bell earned his reputation as the Kansas City Chiefs' most innovative practical joker when he found a way to strand Hank Stram on top of his beloved cherry picker — a crane-like device that allowed the coach to view his entire team from above the practice field.

However, Jan Stenerud proved he had his own unique sense of humor when he became the first true place kicker inducted into the Pro Football Hall of Fame.

"I went to Montana State on a ski-jumping scholarship," the native of Norway quipped, "but my greatest

**66 I went to Montana State on a ski-jumping scholarship, but my greatest jump of all was to the Hall of Fame. 99**

*– Chiefs Hall of Fame kicker Jan Stenerud*

jump of all was to the Hall of Fame.

"I know that when I got a note that I was one of the 15 finalists (for possible induction), I knew I was in a position that nobody had been in before. So I didn't know what to expect at all. It was total uncharted territory. I got enough votes the first time I was eligible and I thought it was very exciting and I was very proud of it."

*On the opening kickoff, he put the ball through the goal posts and seven rows deep into the bleachers. I had seen all I needed to see.*

Stenerud and the Chiefs were a match made in football heaven.

"We drafted Jan as a future choice in 1966," Stram said, "but I wanted to see the kid in person so I went to see a game in Tulsa. On the opening kickoff, he put the ball through the goal posts and seven rows deep into the bleachers. I had seen all I needed to see."

Stenerud signed with the Chiefs and, 19 years later, would retire as the most prolific and successful kicker in the history of the game.

"Now, what you have to remember about Jan is that back then, special teams guys didn't get much practice," said Chiefs quarterback Len Dawson, who held for Stenerud on field goals. "There weren't any domed stadiums or kicking nets to practice with on the sidelines. This guy was way, way ahead of his time.

"I think he kicked a 54-yarder in the first game against Houston and we all thought we really had something special."

That year Stenerud led the AFL with 21 field goals. Stenerud always gave credit to Stram, who made sure the newcomer to football felt at ease and appreciated.

"Coach brought me in a month early before my first season," Stenerud said. "Every day he had me out there kicking 50 balls, and he was doing all the holding. It was Coach Stram who pointed out that I was more likely to miss a field goal from the right hash mark. I didn't realize that but his charts showed me it was true. He had me practice from that side until it was no longer a problem."

It took a while for opposing coaches to find out about the young man from Norway.

One visiting coach at Municipal Stadium couldn't figure out what all the white X markings were on the wall that was 10 yards behind the goal post in the west end zone.

Finally, he asked Chiefs groundskeeper George Toma about the strange markings.

Toma just smiled and said, ""Those are the spots where Stenerud's kickoffs have hit the fence."

The coach just shook his head and went about his pregame routine, knowing that Stenerud would likely play a key role in another Chiefs victory.

Stenerud's run to the Hall of Fame would make a nice Ripley's Believe It Or Not feature.

"I was on the ski team and part of the work-out was always running the stadium steps at Montana State," Stenerud said. "And while the ski team would run the stadium steps, a couple of the football players would kick extra points down on the field. And I went down and kicked a few with the toe, like everybody kicked it in those days. And I asked them if I could kick with the side of my foot, like they take a corner kick in soccer, and they said 'Yes, yes you can.' So I started kicking a few with the side of my foot."

Montana State basketball coach Roger Craft was watching this sophomore ski jumper bomb kick after kick, so he sought out football coach Jim Sweeney.

"Coach Sweeney saw me a couple of weeks later running the stadium steps and he hollered at me and said 'Hey, get down here. I hear you can kick.' So I kicked a few in front of the team. And they thought I had a chance, and they decided I should go out for spring practice. So I went out for spring practice my senior year and made the team."

Not only did he make the team, he made collegiate history by kicking what was then the longest NCAA field goal ever (59 yards).

Stenerud kicked 18 of 33 field goals in two years at MSU. His percentage might have been better if Sweeney had had a reliable punter. The coach would often send Stenerud into kick an unmakeable field goal attempt, rather than punt the ball a few yards down the field.

"My mother was a little leery of my playing football," Stenerud said, "and my father hoped I would jump for Norway in the Winter Olympics."

Stenerud revolutionized the AFL, in much the same way Wilt Chamberlain changed basketball. The 7-foot-1 giant was so dominant that the NBA elected to widen the lane, introduce offensive goaltending, and revise rules governing in-bounding the ball.

Because Stenerud's kickoffs were sailing into the stands, the line from which the ball was kicked was moved from the 40, to the 35, and eventually to the 30.

He scored 1,699 points and held the career record with 373 successful field goals, 38 more than previous leader George Blanda.

In 1969, he kicked 16 straight field goals, eclipsing the existing pro mark of 13 straight held by Cleveland's Hall of Famer, Lou Groza. He ranked second with 17 field goals of more than 50 yards – his longest was a 55-yarder against Denver in 1970. His 580 career points-after-touchdown place him third in that category.

The personable kicker played in two AFL All-Star games and four AFC-NFC Pro Bowls. He was named the Most Valuable Player of the 1972 Pro Bowl when he kicked four field goals, including a then-record 48-yarder, and two extra points.

# He Left His Mark on All of Us – The One and Only Marcus Allen

When Marcus Allen scored a touchdown, he found the official in the end zone and handed him the ball.

The Hall of Fame running back went into the pro football shrine as a member of the Kansas City Chiefs, despite enjoying many of his glory years as a member of the Oakland Raiders. He brought a presence that still lingers in the Arrowhead Stadium locker room. His style and class were reminiscent of the league's earlier years.

"When Marcus scored," former Chiefs fullback Kimble Anders said, "he would hand the ball to the official and trot off the field. He acted like he had been there before. You just don't see that anymore."

The antics of some of today's younger players don't sit well with Allen.

"I was pretty quiet when I first came into the league," Allen said. "I knew it was important to keep my mouth shut and prove myself. I thought before I talked. Now I think it is the other way around.

"It's just a different attitude. You see a different attitude, a changing of the guard."

While he is no fan of showboating or taunting, Allen confesses that he still loves the game.

"It's my DNA. The football field is a great place to find out about yourself, to challenge yourself," he said. "There are a tremendous amount of

Photo courtesy of Scott E. Thomas Photography

obstacles you must face in your life and football is the perfect forum for working through them."

Allen learned the game in his back yard. He had just watched fellow Hall of Famer LeRoy Kelly run roughshod over an opponent in the muddy fields at Cleveland's Municipal Stadium.

"We watched it on television, and my brothers and I would always go out and try the same moves we'd seen in a game," Allen said. "We didn't have a lot of grass but we had a lot of dirt, and we watered down the backyard. And, as a result of that, I learned how to play in the mud and never had any trepidation about bad weather."

He didn't face many muddy fields at USC, where he became the first collegiate back to ever rush for 2,000 yards in a single season. But that lofty mark didn't make much of an impact with NFL scouts.

Although Allen set the NCAA single-season rushing record (2,342 yards) and had the most 200-yard rushing games in history (eight), coaches and scouts were questioning his speed, durability and toughness.

"I didn't understand it then," Allen said, "and I still don't understand it."

When draft day arrived, Darrin Nelson of Stanford and Arizona State's Gerald Riggs were selected in front of Allen, who slipped all the way to the 10th pick, where he was finally tabbed by the Oakland Raiders.

He didn't make a big scene or downgrade those players drafted before him. He simply went out and earned Rookie of the Year honors in 1982 and went on to claim both NFL and Super Bowl MVP awards. He once rushed for 100 or more yards in 11 consecutive games, an NFL mark that stood for 10 years.

> *It was the most humiliating thing I'd*
> *ever had to endure.*

But Allen soon found himself at odds with Oakland team owner Al Davis, and he was looking for a fresh start. Allen rushed for just 301 and 287 yards in the two seasons before he signed with the Chiefs as an unrestricted free agent in 1993.

"It was the most humiliating thing I'd ever had to endure," Allen said of his final go-around with the Raiders. "Marty and the Chiefs gave me the shot in the arm I needed at that time in my career."

Allen was a longtime favorite of Chiefs head coach Marty Schottenheimer, who believed the back's lack of carries in his two previous seasons would result in great success in Kansas City.

"He's easily identified because of his greatness," Schottenheimer said, "his performances in the past. The thing that you have to appreciate about Marcus Allen is that you can place him in the role he has been cast and know there will be no change in the way he works, the way he prepares, the way he is going to set an example for others to follow."

While a member of the Chiefs, Allen became the only man in the history of the NFL to rush for 10,000 yards and catch passes totaling 5,000 yards.

Not a bad accomplishment for a player who earned little respect on draft day.

"Achieving that goal was meaningful," Allen said, "because when I first came into the league there was a string of articles saying I wouldn't be very good, I wouldn't last very long and would only be an average player."

As a former Houston Oilers coach said about his prize running back, Earl Campbell, "He may not be in a class by himself, but it don't take long to call roll."

The same can be said of Marcus Allen.

# Thomas Sacked Quarterbacks and Illiteracy in Kansas City

Derrion Thomas knows a thing or two about pressure. The Blue Springs South High School graduate led his team to the Class 6 state championship football game in 2008 with a five-sack performance in a 14-9 upset victory over defending state champion Rockhurst.

But that was nothing compared to the pressure he would feel when he helped induct his father Derrick Thomas into the Pro Football Hall of Fame.

"I spent all summer working on my dad's Hall of Fame acceptance speech," said Thomas, who wore his father's No. 58 shoulder pads in that memorable win over Rockhurst.

"I worked on it a little bit at a time. I know a lot of people are going to be at Canton for the Hall of Fame induction and a lot more are going to be watching on television, so I want it to be perfect."

Photo courtesy of Scott E. Thomas Photography

Derrion said he's not sure what tone his speech will take, although he has to deliver it in three to five minutes.

"My mom has been talking to the Hall of Fame and so far, all I know is that it can't be over five minutes, so that's what I'm working on – a five-minute speech that tells people what my dad meant to me and the Chiefs," Derrion said.

During the heyday of the Chiefs, a team that won more home games than any other NFL team during the 1990s, Derrick Thomas defined a squad that used defense as its calling card.

"With my dad, and Neil (Smith, the All-Pro defensive end and Blue Springs resident), those teams were pretty

> **" I was at the game where my dad got seven sacks. On the ride home, we didn't talk about the game at all. We just talked about other stuff like how I was doing in school – things like that. "**
> *– DERRION THOMAS, talking about his dad, Derrick Thomas*

good," said Derrion, who was a third grader at Notre Dame de Sion when his father was injured in an automobile accident in 1999 as he drove to Kansas City International Airport to catch a flight to St. Louis to watch the NFC Championship game.

As a result of that accident, the nine-time Pro Bowl player was paralyzed from the chest down and later died from a blood clot that traveled to his lungs.

"We had seats on the front row, on the 50-yard line, right behind the Chiefs bench (at Arrowhead)," Derrion said. "My dad would get me after games and take me into the locker room and we'd ride home and talk about everything but football. I know how much football meant to him, and I'm so happy that he was finally inducted into the Hall of Fame. I've had so many talks with Neil over the years, and we couldn't figure out why it took five years.

"But now that he's going to be inducted, well, it's going to be very special for everyone in our family."

Derrion said he will donate the No. 58 pads to the Hall of Fame.

"When I wore those pads, I felt like my dad was with me," Derrion said. "But now, those pads are going to the Hall of Fame. It's going to be an amazing experience. Inside, I'm going to be bawling like a little baby. But outside, I'm going to be cool and calm – just like my dad."

His father redefined the linebacking role for the Kansas City Chiefs as general manager Carl Peterson and coach Marty Schottenheimer made Thomas, an All-America from Alabama, their first-ever No. 1 draft pick. Thomas, the 1988 Butkus Award winner, was named the best linebacker in the college ranks. He followed that honor by winning the NFL Defensive Rookie of the Year Award.

He also earned the first of nine consecutive Pro Bowl berths, becoming the first Kansas City rookie to make the Pro Bowl since running back Joe Delaney in 1981. He was the first Chiefs outside linebacker to earn a spot in that game since Pro Football Hall of Famer Bobby Bell in 1973.

In true Thomas fashion, when he arrived at the Pro Bowl he found that he had been issued jersey No. 59, instead of his familiar No. 58. The numbered jerseys are handed out through seniority, so Thomas gave his first Pro Bowl jersey to a neighbor back in Independence, Missouri, and said, "You keep this one. I'll keep all the ones with No. 58 on them."

It took the Chiefs just two seasons before they made the NFL playoffs. In just his second season, he set the NFL afire and created fear among opposing quarter-backs as he recorded 20 sacks, the fifth-highest total in NFL history.

Perhaps his finest individual performance came on Veteran's Day, Nov. 11, 2000, when he set an NFL single-game mark of seven sacks in a 17-16 home loss to Seattle. On the final play of the game, Seahawks quarterback Dave Krieg, who would later become

Thomas' teammate with the Chiefs, eluded his grasp and found Paul Skansi alone in the end zone for a game-winning 25-yard score.

Thomas had dedicated the game to his father, Robert, an Air Force pilot who lost his life during a mission called Operation Linebacker II in Vietnam.

When presented with the seventh-sack football, Thomas called a friend in the locker room over to his stall and tossed him the ball.

"I don't keep anything from a loss," said Thomas, who later added, "I was on a mission today. I read in the paper that Derrick Thomas was in a sack slump."

Thomas led the Chiefs in sacks his first four seasons. In 1991 he became the first linebacker to win the team's MVP Award. That was the same year he started "The Third and Long Foundation," a nationally-renowned reading program for inner-city youth in Kansas City. He wanted to sack illiteracy in the metro area, so Thomas would spend Saturday afternoons during the regular season reading with youngsters at libraries. His enthusiasm sparked the reading habits of countless young students throughout the Midwest.

"As good a player as Derrick was," said his best friend and teammate Neil Smith, "he was an even better person. A lot of guys start programs and the like, and they just lend their name to them. Derrick didn't do that. He went out and read with the kids and showed them how important it was to study and work hard in school. And when Derrick Thomas is telling a kid that, they listen."

Thomas was making a name for himself in the NFL and in his community. He and Smith became one of the

Photo courtesy of Scott E. Thomas Photography

most feared pass rushing tandems in the NFL and they paved the way to an AFC West division title in 1993.

The Chiefs made a thrilling run through the playoffs. They upset the red-hot Houston Oilers, who had won 11 straight games, to advance to the first AFC Championship Game in franchise history.

"That was a special season for a lot of reasons," Thomas said. "Joe (Montana) came over to play quarterback and we had an offense and a defense that really complemented each other. It was a lot of fun. There was no place I'd rather be than Arrowhead Stadium on a Sunday afternoon with the stands full and the fans chanting and doing the Arrowhead chop."

Thomas earned the NFL's Man of the Year Award that season, and the following season his teammates again named him the team MVP.

"For me, my goals are a lot higher than just being a successful linebacker or being All-Pro," Thomas said. "When my career is over, I want people to look back and view me as the best, or one of the two best to ever play the position."

# They Made Us Proud

THEY MADE US PROUD

# Otis Taylor:
# On the Verge of Greatness

In Kansas City, it's simply called "the catch."

It came in a game against the Washington Redskins, in which Otis Taylor made a terrific one-handed catch of a 28-yard touchdown pass from quarterback Len Dawson to seal a 27-20 victory for the Chiefs.

"I know I'll never forget it," said Dawson. "Otis made my job so easy. If I got it close, Otis caught it.

"Everyone remembers that catch, and it was a great one because the defender had Otis' other hand pinned to his side, and the only way he can catch it is with one hand.

"But on the previous play, he made an even better catch. He's on the sidelines and I'm trying to throw the ball away and he reaches out and makes this great one-handed catch.

"After the game, reporters are asking me about the play and there was no way I'm going to tell them I was throwing it away. I told them I put it right where Otis could catch it. Actually, anyplace you put it, he'd catch it."

Taylor made key receptions for the Chiefs in back-to-back playoff wins over the New York Jets and Oakland Raiders following the 1969 season.

"Against New York, Otis told me the safety was guarding him and he couldn't keep up with him," Dawson said, "so we went with a deep pattern that was a bit dangerous because of the way the wind was swirling in Shea Stadium.

"I threw the ball and for a moment, I thought I'd overthrown it, but Otis had a gear other receivers didn't have and he took off and caught it. It set up a touchdown pass to Gloster Richardson and we won the game, 13-6. Otis telling me about that play made the difference in the game."

The Chiefs needed a win at Oakland to secure a trip to the Super Bowl, and Taylor made sure it happened.

"Whenever we needed a big play, Otis came up with it," Dawson said. "I hit him on a 35-yard play from our 2 and that got us out of a hole. We eventually scored the go-ahead touchdown and won the game 17-7."

Taylor's most memorable play was also one of the biggest plays in Kansas City history. It came in Super Bowl IV against the Minnesota Vikings. Dawson hit Taylor on a short swing pass and he broke free along the sidelines. One of the biggest and strongest wide receivers in the history of the AFL broke away from Minnesota's Earsell Mackbee at the 40-yard line and stiff-armed Karl Kassulke inside the 10 to complete a 46-yard touchdown that iced the Chiefs' victory.

"I knew the game was over right then," Dawson said. "He was such a great wide receiver, and he was a great athlete. There was no one like him back in the days of the AFL. If we had thrown the ball more to him, he would have owned every record there was."

Taylor said back then, "I knew we needed to score because I remember the way Minnesota came back against the (Los Angeles) Rams. I got hit, but spun away from the first guy. Then I hit the last guy with my hand. I always try to punish a defender, just like they try to punish me."

Many of Taylor's teammates believe he should be alongside Dawson and the other Chiefs greats in the Pro Football Hall of Fame.

"Otis is a Hall of Famer in every sense of the word," Dawson said. "He could do it all. He was a great receiver and a great blocker. We scored a lot of rushing touchdowns off Otis Taylor blocks."

Taylor retired with the most receiving yards (7,306) and receiving touchdowns (57) in Chiefs history. Even though he is not in the Hall of Fame, he considers himself a lucky man.

"I am so fortunate that I got to play in Kansas City," Taylor said. "It was a great time in my life."

# Mike Garrett

Mike Garrett was a small running back who always seemed to come up with the big run.

He stood just 5'9" and weighed 200 pounds, but as quarterback Len Dawson said, "When we needed a big running play, we gave the ball to the little man who always got the job done."

When he signed with the Chiefs in 1966, Garrett, the Heisman Trophy winner from USC, was accustomed to the bright lights and glamour of Southern California. And he made sure the lights were bright in Kansas City as he played a pivotal role in the team's Super Bowl victory.

"Coach (Hank) Stram would come up with these creative game plans and you knew that every time you touched the ball, you had the chance to do something special," said Garrett.

Garrett scored on runs of 1 and 18 yards in the Chiefs' AFL championship victory over Buffalo, and he put Super Bowl IV against the Minnesota Vikings out of reach with a 5-yard touchdown carry.

He was an All-AFL selection in 1967 when he rushed for 1,087 yards and nine touchdowns and was a member of the AFL All-Star teams in 1967 and 1968.

"He might make a 10- or 12-yard run, and run 20 or 30 yards to get the yardage," Dawson said. "He was just unstoppable in the open field and a lot of fun to watch."

In just five seasons, he rushed for 3,246 yards and scored 23 touchdowns, proving that good things come in small packages.

# Chris Burford

Chris Burford was about as flashy as a T-shirt and a pair of jeans. While his fellow wide receiver Otis Taylor earned much of the attention, Burford was content to come up with the big play when the Chiefs needed it.

Burford, who looked like a Marine Corps recruit with his spit-and-polish crew cut, wasn't fast or especially physical, and he couldn't jump tall buildings in a single bound.

"What made Chris so special," quarterback Len Dawson said, "were his hands and the way he ran a route. He could catch anything. That's because he was always in the perfect position to make a catch. You didn't have to improvise with Chris; you just threw the ball and he was right there where he was supposed to be."

*If Al Davis takes off his leisure suit in the woods, do the Raiders still suck?*

The Stanford product was at his best near the sidelines, where he would cradle a ball in his arms, while somehow keeping his feet inbounds.

"If you work hard enough at something," Burford said, "you usually get pretty good at it. And we had the best quarterback in the league in Lenny. I'm happy to know that I inspired him because he certainly inspired me."

When Burford retired in 1967, he was the team's all-time leading receiver with 391 receptions for 5,505 yards and 55 touchdowns.

"We spent a lot of time after practice working on routes," Dawson said, "and it all paid off. You would see him make a catch and the defensive back would just shake his head in disgust."

## Walt Corey

Walt Corey sits on the front porch of his fashionable Lee's Summit, Missouri, home, blowing steel-blue smoke rings that disappear over his manicured lawn and flower garden.

The former AFL All-Star linebacker starred for the Dallas Texans and Kansas City Chiefs. Although he's 71

Walt Corey

Photo courtesy of Scott E. Thomas Photography

years old now, he still looks like he's chiseled from granite and he's wearing a T-shirt that asks: Do I Look Like a People Person?

No, he looks like a former football player who could still strap on the pads and show today's kids a thing or two.

"Smokey," Corey says, as he talks to his former Texans and Chiefs teammate Smokey Stover on a cell phone, "can you believe it's been 50 years since we started playing pro ball?

"Fifty years – my God that seems like a long time ago."

The two members of the elite AFL/NFL fraternity talk about the old days before Corey lays the phone on a table, takes a sip of black coffee, and says, "I'll never forget our first camp. We were at Roswell, New Mexico, with no water breaks and two-a-day practices in what seemed like 110-degree heat.

"Hank (Stram) would line guys up for one-on-one drills and if you lost, you went home. We went with 100 guys and came home with 33. When practice was over, they had these irrigation ditches and we all ran over and jumped in them.

"We slept in cots at a military school, got up the next morning, and did it all over again."

Corey pauses for a moment, takes a long drag on his cigar and adds, "And we loved it. We weren't playing for the money. I made $6,500 a year – played nine years in the league and made a total of about $65,000, counting bonuses. But the money wasn't that important back then.

"It's like talking to Smokey today. We all keep in touch. We weren't just teammates. We were family."

## Fred Arbanas

Walt Corey loves to talk about his former Kansas City Chiefs teammates.

Corey, a linebacker, was tougher than a $1 steak, so when he calls Fred Arbanas a "player's player," you know the all-time AFL tight end has been paid the ultimate compliment.

"Freddy could have played any position on the offensive line," Corey said. "He was as strong as a guard or tackle and he had the hands of a wide receiver. He's another guy who should be in the Hall of Fame."

The Michigan State grad starred on two Super Bowl teams and retired with 198 receptions and 3,101 yards – both tight end records until Tony Gonzalez came along.

"Fred was a man's man," Len Dawson said. "He was the guy who brought his lunch box to work, punched the time clock and gave it everything he had every down."

*Hank Stram had placed a patch over his own left eye and had his sons toss him a football as he ran Arbanas' routes in the back yard.*

Arbanas could have been the poster boy for the old American Football League.

When the Chiefs hammered the NFL's Chicago Bears 66-24 in an exhibition game following their loss to the Green Bay Packers in the first Super Bowl, Chiefs owner Lamar Hunt heard Arbanas say, "That's the one win I will always remember."

The big tight end threw many key blocks in the Chiefs' 23-7 win over Minnesota in Super Bowl IV.

That was a great moment in Chiefs history, but it paled in comparison to the victory he experienced when he overcame the loss of an eye – the result of a mugging in downtown Kansas City.

"I was lying in a hospital bed convinced my football career was over," said Arbanas, a six-time All-AFL tight end. "I left the hospital and went to practice and my eye started to hemorrhage. I had to have an operation and lost the sight in that eye and I thought my football career was over."

Little did Arbanas know that Chiefs coach Hank Stram had placed a patch over his own left eye and had his sons toss him a football as he ran Arbanas' routes in the back yard.

"I wanted to see if Freddy could still see the ball," Stram explained. "When I did that, I realized he could still see the ball and I was going to give him every opportunity to come back to the team."

While he recovered, Arbanas played catch with his son, and he too found out he could follow the flight of the ball with just one eye.

"I met Hank and Lenny at our training facility and Hank told me he knew I could play again. And after a while, I began to believe him."

After hours of extra sessions with Dawson, Arbanas regained his confidence and enjoyed six more years in the NFL.

# Jerry Mays

Jerry Mays was AFL through and through.

"I loved the AFL," said Mays, a heralded defensive lineman who retired in 1970 following the Chiefs' win in Super Bowl IV.

"It was part of me and the merger with the NFL made it easier to retire. I know it was a business decision, but it took a lot of fun out of it. I was AFL from start to finish, proud of the league, tickled to death I'd played in it. It was always the little guy against the big guy and I liked that."

While he didn't overpower many opponents, Mays used his agility and quick feet to throw a stunned running back for a loss or sack a quarterback at a key moment in the game.

"He just loved to play," Len Dawson said. "I think Jerry Mays would have played for free."

The late defensive end's teammates agree.

"God he loved the game," linebacker Bobby Bell said. "He came to play every down, every game. We just called him 'the captain.'"

Mays stood 6'4" and weighed "only" 240 pounds, but he often said, "You can't measure a man's heart."

"Jerry was the only man I ever coached," Hank Stram said, "who could play at an all-star level at every position on the line."

Mays was named to the All-Time AFL All-Star team and was All-AFL as a defensive tackle two times and as an end four times.

Mays lost a long battle with cancer in 1994.

## Jerrell Wilson

How good was Chiefs punter Jerrell Wilson?

"You can't compare any other punter to Jerrell Wilson," Chiefs coach Hank Stram said. "That wouldn't be fair."

His nickname was "Thunderfoot," and he saved the Chiefs on many occasions with his booming punts inside an opponent's 10-yard line.

"He was amazing," Dawson said. "He was just so powerful. He did things you just don't see anymore."

Wilson starred for the Chiefs for 15 seasons, and was named the All-Time All-AFL punter. He owns team records for the most punts (1,018), average in a career (43.4), a season (46.1) and a game (56.4). He had four career punts over 70 yards and was named to three Pro Bowl teams following the AFL-NFL merger in 1970.

Wilson passed away in 2005.

# Ed Budde

How does a guard become the AFL's Offensive Player of the Week?

"When that guard is Ed Budde, that's a pretty easy question to answer," quarterback Len Dawson said. "Mr. Budde made my life pretty easy for several years."

Budde's performance in a 24-10 Chiefs' win against Oakland in 1968 made him the first interior lineman to ever win the weekly award in the history of the NFL.

In that game, coach Hank Stram threw an old T-formation offense at the Raiders and the Chiefs gained 215 yards on the ground in the first half alone. Budde and tackle Jim Tyrer were credited with blocking on 111 of those yards.

"I've never seen a guard play like that," right tackle Dave Hill said. "It was the best game an offensive lineman can have."

Added tight end Fred Arbanas, "No guard can play like that."

No one appreciated Budde's performance more than Dawson.

"Ed was amazing," Dawson said. "He's another guy who should be in the Hall of Fame. He was just the best. And he was the best for 14 years."

The Michigan State product was part of an amazing 1963 draft class that included Bobby Bell and Buck Buchanan, two future Hall of Famers.

Budde started 14 years for the Chiefs. He appeared in six AFL All-Star games, six NFL Pro Bowl games, and started on two Super Bowl teams.

He stood 6-5 and weighed 260 pounds and dominated his position like no other player during his era.

# E.J. Holub

*I look like I lost a knife fight with a midget.*

E.J. Holub holds a distinct record in the NFL.

The Chiefs' all-time great is the only player in the history of the league to start two Super Bowls at two different positions.

He was a starting linebacker in the first Super Bowl and was quarterback Len Dawson's center in Super Bowl IV. With his Texas twang, his 10-gallon cowboy hat, and a walk that made him look like he just got off a buckin' bronco, Holub was one of a kind.

"You just hear the mention of his name and you smile," Dawson said. "He was a fiery competitor who loved the game, but during his 10-year career, he had nine knee operations. And that was long before anyone knew about the arthroscopic variety."

"I look like I lost a knife fight with a midget," Holub said, as he placed a wad of chewing tobacco into his mouth. "But dad gummit, it was worth every minute of it."

Those operations have taken a toll on the likeable Texan, who has had a total of 18 surgeries and today has an artificial hip that allows him to ride the ponies on his Oklahoma ranch and get in the occasional round of golf.

Holub was a five-time AFL All-Star at linebacker, who had to change positions to center after he tore his hamstring in 1967.

"I didn't have any mobility after I tore my hamstring," he said. "Heck, I could put up with the knee operations. Drain a little fluid off before the game and I was ready to go. But that hamstring was a different kind of injury. But I didn't let it keep me from playing."

Holub was known as the "Holler Guy," because he was always on the sidelines encouraging his teammates.

"No one gave more to the game than E.J.," Dawson said. "You'd see him in the training room and think there's no way he could play and he comes out and has a great game. I think that's why the fans always loved him so much."

## Jim Tyrer

Mention the name Jim Tyrer to anyone associated with the Chiefs during his NFL reign as the best tackle on the planet, and a sad smile comes to their face.

"I miss him every day," said Bob Johnson, who rode the Chiefs' mascot, War Paint, around Municipal Stadium and Arrowhead Stadium following every Chiefs' touchdown. "He was a big ol' boy, with the best personality and a great smile. He'd come over to my place and play softball with the guys and he had such a good time."

Tyrer passed away in 1980, and he is still missed.

"When they made Jim Tyrer," coach Hank Stram said, "they broke the mold. He was the tackle you judged every other tackle against. He was the best."

Another member of the All-Time AFL team, Tyrer was selected to nine AFL or NFL all-star teams and started an amazing 180 consecutive games, never missing the call to battle during his 13-year career.

**What do you call a San Diego Charger with a Super Bowl ring?**

**A thief.**

"He made it look easy," said Chiefs running back Mike Garrett, the beneficiary of countless Tyrer blocks. "He would take on two blockers and open this huge hole."

Tyrer threw the block that sprung Garrett for a decisive touchdown in Super Bowl IV.

"With the amount of strain during that game, it took me nearly a week to sit down and realize what we had accomplished," Tyrer said. "There was so much leading up to that game. I think the big plus was that we had been there before (as the AFL representative to the first Super Bowl three years before). There was great pressure playing for our league against the NFL."

Tyrer stood 6'6" and weighed 270 pounds, which made him one of the biggest linemen of his generation.

"Jim could block out the sun," quarterback Len Dawson said. "I was so happy he was on my side. Jim was just massive. There were never two better offensive linemen on the same team than Jim and Ed (Budde). I just don't understand why they aren't in the Hall of Fame."

# Jim Lynch

Many people believe Jim Lynch should be in the Pro Football Hall of Fame.

"Jim would be in the Hall of Fame," said former Chiefs linebacker Walt Corey, "if he hadn't played alongside the two best in the history of the AFL – Bobby Bell and Willie Lanier. It's easy to get overlooked when you play with those two guys."

Lynch starred for 11 years for the Chiefs and retired the same day as his Hall of Fame teammate and friend, Lanier.

"Jim was a great, great linebacker," said Lanier, who followed Bell into the Hall of Fame to become just the second Chiefs player to gain such an honor. "He was overlooked, and that's a shame because he could do it all."

But Lynch has no complaints.

"It's just an honor to be mentioned in the same breath with Bobby Bell and Willie Lanier," said Lynch, who was the co-captain of Notre Dame's 1966 national championship team.

"I played with two of the best linebackers in the history of the game for eight seasons (1967-74) and have many great memories."

While he is not a member of the pro hall of fame, Lynch was inducted into the College Hall of Fame in 1992.

*"With his Texas twang, his 10-gallon cowboy hat, and a walk that made him look like he just got off a buckin' bronco, E. J. Holub was one of a kind."*

# Johnny Robinson

Johnny Robinson was one of the best all-around athletes in the history of the Kansas City Chiefs.

He led the team in interceptions from his safety position and finished with 58 career thefts, which at the time was sixth in NFL history (he was third all-time in the AFL) and he is a member of the All-Time All-AFL team.

"When we needed a big interception to turn the game around, we looked to Johnny," Len Dawson said of his former roommate. "He just had a knack for making big plays."

Dawson recalls a conversation the two friends had leading up to Super Bowl IV.

"The Vikings were heavily favored and I asked Johnny if he thought we could beat them and he said, 'Heck yes.' That was good enough for me."

The Chiefs claimed a 23-7 victory and Robinson extinguished any last-gasp attempt by the Vikings to make a late comeback with an interception.

As he sat on the ground clutching the ball, Robinson thrust his fist and index finger into the air to signify that the Chiefs were No. 1.

While he was a star in the AFL and NFL, Robinson went on to enjoy a much greater calling when he retired in 1971.

The former member of the 1959 LSU national championship football team opened his sprawling Monroe, Louisiana, home to troubled youths – many of whom simply called him "Dad."

# Deron Cherry

How's this for a Hollywood script? A punter tries out for an NFL team and becomes one of the top free safeties in the history of the league.

Nah, no one would ever believe it.

"Well they better believe it," a grinning Deron Cherry said, "because it's true. I don't know about being one of the top safeties in league history, but I loved my time playing for the Chiefs."

Cherry was a six-time Pro Bowl free safety and the premier defensive back of the 1980s.

"I don't know of a better one," said Len Dawson, the Chiefs Hall of Fame quarterback. "We had some great backs in the 1980s and no one was better than Deron."

Cherry wasn't sure if he could make it in the NFL when his former defensive coach at Rutgers, Ted Cottrell, joined the staff of Chiefs coach Marv Levy.

"Ted called me and asked if I had ever signed with anyone," Cherry said. "I told him Cleveland was getting ready to offer me a contract and he told me to get on a plane and come to Kansas City before I signed anything."

Cherry tried out as a punter, but didn't make the final cut. When he turned his playbook into Levy he reminded the coach that he had played in the Rutgers secondary.

"I was disappointed when I was cut," Cherry said, "but I knew I could play in the NFL."

When veteran strong safety Herb Christopher was injured in the first game of the 1981 season, the Chiefs called Cherry.

"I was part of a secondary that included Gary Green, Gary Barbaro and Eric Harris," Cherry said. "I was playing with the best players of their time."

Barbaro soon signed a free-agent contract to play in the USFL and Cherry became the starting safety on one of the game's top defensive units.

"I know there were skeptics," he said, "but I had faith in my ability. I never wanted to just make the roster. I wanted to start and be considered one of the best players on the team."

One of Cherry's finest moments came during the 1985 season when he intercepted Seattle's Dave Krieg four times in a 28-7 Chiefs victory.

The four interceptions tied the NFL single-game record.

"The one thing I remember about that game," Cherry said, "was catching the four balls. But I also remember not catching a ball the five other times I had a chance for an interception."

Another memorable moment for Cherry came in 1990, when he battled back from a severe knee injury to rejoin his teammates in a game against the Los Angeles Raiders.

"There were times I thought about giving up," Cherry said, "because the pain was unbearable. It brought tears to my eyes. I kept asking myself, 'Is it worth it?' And I kept answering, 'Yes.'"

The hard work paid off in a 9-7 victory over the Raiders when he made a jarring tackle on Bo Jackson and knocked the ball loose. It was recovered by Albert Lewis, and kicker Nick Lowery followed with a field goal.

Teammate Derrick Thomas said at the time, "The man let that play make his statement. Deron Cherry is back."

When he retired in 1991, he was third on the Chiefs' all-time list for interceptions (50) and led the team in tackles four times and interceptions six times.

# Nick Lowery

Nick Lowery, the Kansas City Chiefs' all-time scoring leader (1,466), will forever be known as the kicker who replaced Hall of Fame legend Jan Stenerud.

But Lowery failed 11 times before finally landing a spot with the Chiefs.

*I ran into a Chargers fan the other day. Then, I backed up and ran into him again.*

"After I was cut by the New York Jets for the second time, I told myself that I was going to give it one more shot in Kansas City," Lowery said. "At the time, I was able to see that being cut had its healthy side. It prepared me incrementally for the life of a professional football player."

When coach Marv Levy decided to go with the unproven Lowery and give Stenerud a pink slip, fans were aghast. However, Lowery lived up to his coach's expectations and far outlived Levy in Kansas City – playing the next 14 years and earning a spot in the Chiefs Ring of Honor in 2009.

Lowery had the ability to kick a football like few individuals on the planet. But he was not your average jock.

He is the only American to work for President Ronald Reagan on Drug Abuse Policy, and for both President George Bush and President Bill Clinton in the White House Office of National Service.

His Adult Role Models for Youth (ARMY) Program (now known as Youthfriends) used high-profile mentors such as professional athletes to engage more citizens in regular mentoring relationships with inner-city youth in Kansas City, and was recognized by the International YMCA in 1992.

Lowery set all-time NFL records for accuracy and most field goals, was chosen to seven All-NFL teams, and kicked the game-winning points in three NFL Pro Bowls and 15 NFL games.

A graduate of Dartmouth College, Nick is also the first pro athlete to graduate with a Masters from the Harvard University Kennedy School of Government.

Lowery helped launch Americorps in 1993, which brought a domestic Peace Corps challenge to America's communities. In 1995, he was approached by Johns Hopkins Center for American Indian Health to apply his urban-youth ARMY programs to reaching native youth and families. Native Vision is a sports and life skills program that has reached thousands of American Indian youth from over 30 tribes with the help of the NFL Players Association. He is also the founder of Native Vision and Nation Building for Native Youth, two nationally recognized leadership programs, and is vice chair of the National Fund for Excellence in American Indian Education.

# Christian Okoye

*I would be standing on a corner and see men coming at me with machine guns.*

When asked about the pressures that come from being a star running back in the NFL, Christian Okoye simply said, "Pressure? That's not pressure."

As a youngster growing up in Enugu, Nigeria, Okoye recalls the horrors of a civil conflict that tore his country apart.

"I would be standing on a corner and see men coming at me with machine guns," the former Kansas City Chiefs' Pro Bowl running back said. "I would wake up at night and hear gun shots or walk down the street and hide in an alley, fearful that I might be shot and killed. It was a very bad time."

No wonder the man who earned the nickname, "The Nigerian Nightmare," never seemed to be intimidated by opposing defensive players.

"When you went through what I went through," he said, "nothing would scare you. Football was a game. It wasn't war; it was a game."

When Okoye was 6, Ibo insurgents seceded from Nigeria and created the Republic of Biafra. War ravaged Okoye's homeland from 1967 to 1970 and he wondered if he might ever sleep through the night " ... without being awakened by the sound of gunfire."

Okoye grew up to become Africa's top discus (212 feet, 2 inches), hammer throw (219-7), and shot put (59-2) champion.

"I came to the United States to compete in track," Okoye said. "I didn't know what football was until I came to the United States."

That was back in 1982, when he attended tiny Azusa Pacific College in southeast California. He was a seven-time NAIA track champion in four different events, but when he was denied the opportunity to compete in the 1984 Olympics by a group of Nigerian track officials, he decided to try football.

"That was the best choice of my life," Okoye said. "I was so sad when I couldn't compete in the Olympics, and Coach (Jim) Milhon had talked to me about playing football. To me, football meant soccer. I had no idea what it was. I didn't even know how to put on the shoulder pads."

After rushing for -1 yard on two carries in his college debut, he rushed for more than 100 yards in 16 of his next 18 games. His 4.38 speed caught the attention of pro scouts.

When he scored four touchdowns in the Senior Bowl, everyone began to take notice.

"When I saw him on film, my hands began to sweat – he was that exciting," said former Kansas City Chiefs coach Frank Gansz. "He was explosive because of his track training. He was bigger than most of the linemen he played against in college. We just had to teach him the game."

After one intense practice session, a former teammate cried out, "Watch out! Here comes the Nigerian Nightmare."

A nickname was born and a Kansas City sports legend was about to emerge.

In his first NFL game, he carried the ball 21 times for 105 yards.

When coach Marty Schottenheimer took over the team in 1989, he made Okoye the heart and soul of the Chiefs offense and the always-smiling gentleman from Nigeria responded.

"I loved to carry the ball for Marty," Okoye said, smiling. "He called it smash-mouth football. I liked that."

He was a one-man highlight reel ...

Who could forget his 143-yard game against Atlanta, a 153-yard Monday Night Football performance against Miami, or a sizzling touchdown run against Seattle in which seven Seahawks bounced off his rock-hard body?

Former teammate Bill Maas wonders what Okoye might have accomplished had he grown up with the game.

"If he really knew about the game, had that sixth sense that allows the great backs to find the openings, he might have been the best ever," the former defensive lineman said. "As it was, he survived on brute power. He just ran over people. No one – and I mean, no one – wanted to ever get hit by him in practice."

Former center Tim Grunhard echoed that comment.

"If you got hit by Christian from behind, it was like getting hit by a battering ram," Grunhard said. "He'd hit you harder than the opposing defensive linemen. But the man was a player. He was so much fun to block for because you knew if he got any type of opening, he would do the rest."

Injuries began taking their toll on his 6'3", 260-pound frame and he underwent surgery prior to the start of the 1993 season. He retired when he was just 32.

The first player in the history of the Kansas City Chiefs to lead the NFL in rushing (1,480 yards in 1989) capped his short, but brilliant career by earning a spot in the Chiefs Ring of Honor.

# Neil Smith

Neil Smith was ying to Derrick Thomas' yang.

Smith was a member of the NFL's 75th Anniversary team and teamed with Thomas to form one of the most feared pass rushing duos of the 1990s.

The defense that was anchored by Thomas and Smith was a big reason the Chiefs reached postseason play six straight years (1990-96). He left Kansas City in 1996 and went on to win two Super Bowl rings with the Denver Broncos. His Kansas City totals in sacks (86.5) and forced fumbles (29) rank second only to Thomas, the most recent member of the Chiefs organization to make the Pro Football Hall of Fame.

What do you get when a Raiders player sees his shadow?

6 more weeks of bad football.

"I was a No. 1 draft pick in 1988 and I got off to a rough start," said Smith, who was considered a disappointment until coach Marty Schottenheimer came along in 1989 and began working with the budding superstar. "When Derrick got drafted No. 1 in 1989, I kind of took him under my wing. I called him my little buddy and we looked out for each other. We had a lot of fun and experienced a lot of ups and downs, but I loved my time in Kansas City.

"My only regret is that I couldn't help bring the Super Bowl trophy back to Kansas City and Mr. (Lamar) Hunt. When I first stepped foot onto this field, that was my first goal. We never got that done, but we still have some great memories to savor."

# Priest Holmes

Priest Holmes arrived in Kansas City with little fanfare.

But when he became the key that turned the switch of coach Dick Vermeil's explosive offense, he grew into a marquee player and an NFL record holder.

He led the NFL in rushing in 2001 with 1,555 yards and followed that campaign with 1,615 yards in just 14 games in 2002. When it appeared he would likely break Marshall Faulk's single-season touchdown mark of 26, he injured his hip in the 15th game of the 2002 season and had to settle for a league-high 24 scores.

While many experts said the quiet young man from Texas would never rebound from the hip injury he suffered in Denver, he proved them all wrong.

Holmes enjoyed one of the finest seasons in the history of the NFL in 2003 when he rushed for 1,420 yards and scored a then-NFL record 27 touchdowns.

"When you tell Priest he can't do something," former teammate Tony Richardson said, "he's going to prove you wrong. When everyone was saying he won't be back, I knew he'd be back and I knew he'd be better than ever."

Injuries kept Holmes from reaching true NFL greatness and he passed the torch to running back Larry Johnson.

# Larry Johnson

When Herm Edwards replaced Dick Vermeil as the head coach of the Kansas City Chiefs, the first thing he did was address the situation with the team's angry young man.

Edwards called disgruntled running back Larry Johnson, the team's No.1 draft pick in 2002, and told him that he would be the featured back of the Chiefs' offense in 2006.

"He kind of looked at me with this 'Are you messin' with me?' look and I had to assure him that I wasn't messin' with him," Edwards, the former Chiefs head coach said. "He was going to be my running back. If we needed him to carry the ball 30 times a game, we were going to place it in his hands 30 times."

Running back Priest Holmes was a Kansas City favorite and an NFL icon. He had just set the single-season touchdown record and broken nearly every Chiefs rushing record in a six-year span. To complicate matters, future Hall of Fame left tackle Willie Roaf announced his retirement before the start of the 2006 season and quarterback Trent Green went down with a concussion in the season opener and would miss eight games. So all the offensive focus shifted to Johnson.

"I like a challenge and I always said I just wanted the chance to prove what I can do," Johnson said, "and Herman gave me that chance."

Johnson followed up a 1,750-yard season in 2005 with 1,789 yards, 17 touchdowns and a trip to the playoffs in 2006. He was named a member of the AFC Pro Bowl for the second year in a row.

However, injuries, off-field incidents and a new coaching staff might make one wonder about Johnson's future with the team.

"This is a clean slate for the entire group of Kansas City Chiefs as far as I am concerned," new Chiefs coach Todd Haley said, "and I have said that a couple times. We are at ground zero and this is an opportunity for everybody. That is the way myself and my staff are looking at each and every player."

That should be good news for Johnson, who languished on the sidelines his first three years in the league. He knew he had the skills that were necessary to become a star in the NFL, but he had to sit on the bench and wait for his time to come.

He played in just six games in 2003 with no starts, had three starts and 10 games played in 2004, and then came that magical 2005 campaign when Johnson finally got the opportunity to show what he was made of.

Holmes suffered a serious neck injury and the Chiefs placed the ball in the hands of Johnson, who responded with nine consecutive 100-yard games and earned a spot on the AFL Pro Bowl team.

Those are the kinds of numbers he hopes to put up in 2009, the Chiefs' 50th anniversary season.

# Trent Green

Ask former Kansas City Chiefs coach Dick Vermeil for his definition of a leader, and he just might say, "Trent Green."

Green, the former Chiefs quarterback, was a gritty field general who would take a hit, pop up off the turf and return to the huddle with a newfound determination. Over his career, he had to deal with many serious injuries, but they paled in comparison to what he faced in 2005.

His father, and biggest fan, Jim Green, passed away that October.

"I'd never played a game at Arrowhead without my dad there," Green said. "That was very difficult."

Long before any of the fans had arrived at Arrowhead Stadium on the day Green would face the Oakland Raiders in his first game since the death of his father, he walked up to his father's seat and taped a tribute to Jim Green. Some Arrowhead security guards watched Green, and assured the grieving quarterback that no one would sit in his father's seat.

Green then went into the locker room, knowing the Chiefs were about to face their arch-rival, the Raiders. Kansas City played without Pro Bowl left tackle Willie Roaf, Pro Bowl running back Priest Holmes, cornerback Patrick Surtain and reserve defensive backs Jerome Woods and Dexter McCleon, who were all sidelined with injuries.

"We knew we had our leader, Trent Green," defensive back Greg Wesley said, "and we'd follow him anywhere. The guy just lost his father and comes into the game and leads us to the winning touchdown as time expires."

"Now, that's a leader."

The Chiefs managed to claim a thrilling 27-23 win when Larry Johnson, starting in place of Holmes, scored the winning touchdown from 1 yard out as time expired.

"I loved the call," former Chiefs defensive end Jared Allen said, when asked about coach Dick Vermeil's decision to go for the winning touchdown, rather than the chip-shot field goal. "I'm on the sidelines like, 'Yeah! Go for it!' And when we did, I got pretty excited."

So did left guard Brian Waters, who was blocking on the game-winning run.

"We needed to win this game," Waters said. "I was just so proud of every member of this team. The secondary was all beat up and look what they did and we came through with three late scores and get a big win. This is huge."

That's what Green meant to the Kansas City Chiefs.

> What do you call a bunch of Raider fans running down the street?
>
> A jailbreak!

After Johnson scored the game-winning touchdown, Green knelt on the Arrowhead turf and pointed to the heavens.

Tears ran down his face as he embraced Vermeil on the sidelines.

"You want to know what leadership is?" asked Vermeil after the game. "What Trent Green did today, that's leadership."

Green made an impact in Kansas City – but few fans outside the Chiefs' kingdom really know what he meant to the team.

Peyton Manning was the most honored and successful NFL quarterback between 2001 and 2004. He led the Indianapolis Colts to a victory in Super Bowl XLI and threw for 14,287 yards.

Any fantasy football fan would guess that Manning dominated the record books over that period of time.

But few would guess who finished second in passing yards over the same four-season span.

Tom Brady? How about Brett Favre?

Let's see, what other quarterback would rank in their class? Green.

Between 2001 and 2004, Green threw for 12,906 yards.

"I don't look at the yards or the touchdowns or anything like that," said Green. "I look at consistency. That's what is important to me because that's what produces victories."

Green announced his retirement from the NFL following the 2008 season.

# Heroic Act Away from Field Defined Delaney's Legacy

*He could not swim, but that didn't keep him
from trying to help those youngsters.*

Len Dawson has been a big part of the Kansas City
Chiefs as a player and as a broadcaster. Over a career
that spans five decades, he has been involved with and
broadcast countless scenes that leave fans breathless
and begging for more.

But he has seen just one true hero – a man who gave
his life in an attempt to save three small children from
drowning.

That man was former Chiefs running back Joe
Delaney, who died in an attempt to rescue the children
from a water-filled pit in Monroe, Louisiana, in June of
1983.

"Joe was a true hero," Dawson said. "He gave his own
life to try and save those three young men from drowning. He's the hero, not a player who throws a big pass or
runs for a touchdown."

Police officer Marvin Deerman was one of the first
officials on the scene in 1983.

"He saw them get into trouble," Deerman told United
Press International, "and we think he dived in not
knowing how deep the water was and couldn't find the
bottom to push up."

The pit of water was created from heavy rain where a construction crew worked on a waterslide. One boy drowned, one managed to get out of the water, and the other was taken to an emergency room.

Delaney, 24, was from nearby Ruston and was visiting Monroe when he saw the youngsters were in trouble. The pit was right outside an amusement park – its deepest point was 15 feet. Police divers recovered the body of Delaney and the one boy.

Delaney was 5'10" and weighed 184 pounds. He had set a Chiefs' single-season rushing record with 1,121 yards and had the longest run (82 yards) and best single game (193 yards) in the NFL during the 1981 season.

He could not swim, but that didn't keep him from trying to help those youngsters.

"Joe was like a breath of fresh air," Chiefs general manager Jim Schaaf said at the time. "He was so friendly and easy-going and fun to be around. He loved his family, loved life and loved football. He was a special kind of guy."

Delaney was survived by his wife, two daughters and a son.

Delaney was the Chiefs No. 2 draft choice from Northwestern Louisiana University in 1981. He was the AFC Offensive Rookie of the Year and the UPI Rookie of the Year.

"Joe was one of the most well-liked guys on the team," Chiefs defensive back Gary Green said. "That was a shock. Something like that you can never foresee."

Then-team president Jack Steadman said, "So many thoughts go through your mind – of feelings of sorrow for his wife, Carolyn, and other loved ones who were closest to him. Their loss is monumental compared to our loss – and we try to keep that in perspective – but we have lost one of the most exciting players in our history."

The Chiefs honored Delaney's memory by wearing a patch that season that featured his No. 37 and a replica of the President's Medal of Freedom that then-vice president George Bush presented to the Delaney family.

# Will-ingness to Help Others Overshadows Shields' On-Field Stature

He's a lock to gain entry into the Pro Football Hall of Fame on the first ballot, yet his football skills are far down the list when members of the Kansas City Chiefs organization talk about 12-time Pro Bowl offensive lineman Will Shields.

"I don't know of any individual and his wife who have contributed so much and in so many ways to our community," said former Chiefs president and CEO, Carl Peterson.

While Shields' Will to Succeed Foundation is one of the most respected charitable organizations in the area, the 2003 NFL Man of the Year also served on the Board of Directors of the Marillac Center and was the Chiefs United Way spokesperson in 2003.

When asked about his former teammate, Pro Bowl fullback Tony Richardson said, "How much time do you have? I can fill that notebook talking about Will. He is amazing, one of the most amazing men I have ever met. He is an amazing athlete – the way he played 12 years and never missed a game, or even a practice, is remarkable. But as good as he was on the field, he's an even better person."

Another Pro Bowl performer, former quarterback Trent Green, agreed.

"I don't know of many people who have done more for their community than Will and his wife," Green said. "I mean it when I say this: It is an honor to have him as a teammate and a friend. Will Shields is pure class, on and off the playing field."

And former coach Dick Vermeil raves about the veteran lineman. "He's just so smart, and you know he's going to be out there every Sunday. He's a rock – on the field and in the Kansas City community."

The Chiefs have been a longtime supporter of the United Way, and many players have their own charitable endeavors. That made an impact on the third-round pick from Nebraska, who joined the team in 1993.

"When I came here, 17 guys on the team had a foundation," Shields said. "I wanted to do something to help, and I wanted to get totally involved. I didn't just want to lend my name or my face."

His foundation has almost overshadowed his accomplishments on the playing field. When asked how he has time to play football, he just grins. It's the type of smile that can warm a room and make any visitor feel comfortable.

Shields was considered to be the best right guard and the finest all-around lineman in the league.

Numbers have always played an important role in professional sports. Hallowed numbers like 56 (Joe DiMaggio's record hitting streak), 511 (Cy Young's career number of wins), and 100 (Wilt Chamberlain's single-game scoring record) represent greatness.

Numbers also tell a part of Shields' remarkable story. There is 230 – the number of consecutive starts for the 12-time Pro Bowl performer. There is the number 2003 – the year he was named the NFL's Man of the Year.

There is also the number 2005 – the year he and his wife Senia were named Philanthropists of the Year by the Kansas City Council. But think about this number for a moment – 100,000.

That is the number of individuals who have been helped by Shields' Will to Succeed Foundation, which benefits centers for abused and neglected women and children.

When asked what number was special to him, Shields smiled and said, "One. When I came to Kansas City back in 1993, my goal was to help one person. If I could have achieved that goal, I would have been very happy."

Now, he can magnify that happiness by 100,000 – the total number of women and children who have benefited from Shields' charitable work.

# Gonzalez Heads to Atlanta in Search of Super Bowl Ring

*If I am ever fortunate enough to go into the
Hall of Fame, it's going to be as a Chief.*

Tight end Tony Gonzalez has more receptions, more yards, and more touchdowns than any of the previous greats who starred at the position he redefined as a member of the Kansas City Chiefs.

He is a 10-time Pro Bowl player and arguably the most popular Chiefs player of the past decade.

But he never was able to achieve his greatest goal – bringing a championship trophy to the Chiefs fans he loved.

For the remaining years of his career, he's going to be a member of the Atlanta Falcons. New Chiefs General Manager Scott Pioli traded Gonzalez in 2009 to the Falcons for a second-round pick in the 2010 draft.

"I'm going to go on record right now saying I'm going to retire as a Chief," Gonzalez said at a news conference following the trade. "If I am ever fortunate enough to go into the Hall of Fame, it's going to be as a Chief."

"From an organizational standpoint and a personal standpoint there are a lot of mixed emotions here," Pioli said. "I have tremendous personal and professional respect for Tony. He has had a Hall of Fame career on the football field as well as a Hall of Fame career here in the Kansas City community. The teams I was with played against Tony numerous times and he was always a handful.

"He is a tremendous player who you have to take a lot of time to prepare for. I am not going to get into specifics of our conversations with the Falcons other than to say we did not seek to trade Tony; however, there was an opportunity that came to us and after a lot of internal discussions in a short time we decided to make the trade."

First-year head coach Todd Haley backed the general manager's comments.

"I would say it's never easy when you lose a popular player, especially one that has had a career like Tony to this point," Haley said. "That's always difficult. But after a lot of discussions this was the direction we decided to go and was best for the Chiefs now and in the future."

Gonzalez kept his emotions in check during the news conference, jokingly saying, "I'm not retiring. I'm still playing. I'm just leaving a very special place – Kansas City.

"The only regrets I have are things I didn't do. I really wish I could have been a part of something more special. I wanted to be a part of bringing a championship to this city. I got here when I turned 21. I grew up in Kansas City."

"Leaving is going to be sad, real sad. I played for some of the best fans in Kansas City."

But the team never won a playoff game during his Hall of Fame career. He was never able to hoist a championship trophy above his head like other Kansas City sports icons Len Dawson and George Brett.

That's why he's leaving.

He is thrilled and scared to be joining a new team as he enters his 13th season in the NFL.

Why don't they teach driver's education and sex ed at the same time in Denver?

It's too hard on the donkey.

"I have to learn a new offense, meet my new teammates, find a place to live and learn a new freeway system," he said. "But if this were fantasy football, on paper, the Falcons look like a team that could win it all."

He's rich, better looking than most movie stars and has a drop-dead gorgeous wife. He has a home in sunny California and all the bling that goes with being the best in the business.

But he doesn't have the bling that counts the most in the NFL – a Super Bowl ring.

"And getting a ring means everything to me," he said. "I don't need records, I just want to win, and win now. I told the Falcons I don't need to have 95 catches and 10 touchdowns. I'm a competitive guy and I want to win."

# He's No Ordinary Joe:
# A Legend Arrives at Arrowhead

*He looked like a little old man with all these bruises and scars. Then, he'd put on the uniform and become 'Joe Cool.' It was quite a transformation.*

NFL Hall of Famer and legendary Monday Night Football color analyst Frank Gifford eagerly anticipated his broadcast team's visits to Arrowhead Stadium.

"It was like no other stadium," Gifford said. "Once we arrived at Arrowhead and saw the smoke from the grills and smelled the barbeque, we knew we were in Kansas City – and it was special."

He has one special Chiefs memory, but ironically, it didn't take place at Arrowhead Stadium. Denver's Mile High Stadium was the site of a game Gifford, and Chiefs fans, will never forget as an aging Joe Montana proved he still had the magic.

"I'd been doing Monday Night Football for 27 years, and one of the greatest games we ever had was on October 17, 1994 – Denver and Kansas City," Gifford said.

"Joe was 34 for 54 for 393 yards and three touchdowns. And in the final drive he ate up the clock, and with eight seconds remaining hit Willie Davis with the winning touchdown pass which left (Denver quarterback John) Elway with no room to come back. It was a flashback for me because it was clear he was running out of gas, but he had this one more performance for us. I've done well over 400 Monday nights but only a few stick out – and that certainly was one. He was brilliant and it was fun to watch. I've always admired the way he handled his life and himself."

Unfortunately for Chiefs fans, the Montana era ended far too soon.

But for two glorious seasons, "Joe Cool" brought his own special brand of magic to Arrowhead Stadium.

Former Chiefs president and general manager Carl Peterson lured Montana away from the San Francisco 49ers – a team he had led to four Super Bowl titles – so he could finish his career in Kansas City.

"It was really a remarkable time in the history of the franchise," Peterson said. "We all knew Joe was past his prime, but once he arrived, he proved he could still play the game."

Montana led the Chiefs to the AFC Championship Game in his first season and provided some memorable moments that came close to rivaling those he created in San Francisco.

Montana earned the nickname the "Comeback Kid." He was the architect of 31 comeback wins in San Francisco and five in Kansas City.

One of his most memorable wins as a Chiefs ended the Mile High jinx. After that game, Davis lavished praise on Montana.

"He was so cool and confident," the Chiefs wide receiver said. "You just knew with Joe in the huddle, things were going to get done. He was an amazing, amazing quarterback."

Perhaps the most memorable tale of Montana's cool came in the 1989 Super Bowl, where the heavily favored 49ers trailed the Cincinnati Bengals late in the fourth quarter.

Down by three points with 3:20 left in the game, Montana stood in the huddle and said to tackle Harris Barton, "Isn't that John Candy in the stands?"

Photo courtesy of Scott E. Thomas Photography

He then led the 49ers 92 yards, throwing for the winning touchdown with 34 seconds left.

"There have been, and will be, much better arms and legs and much better bodies on quarterbacks in the

NFL," former 49er teammate Randy Cross said, "but if you have to win a game or score a touchdown or win a championship, the only guy to get is Joe Montana."

Former Chiefs linebacker Derrick Thomas was eager to meet Montana when he arrived in Kansas City. But he was a bit surprised the first time he saw the legendary signal caller in the locker room.

"He looked like a little old man with all these bruises and scars," Thomas said, grinning. "Then, he'd put on the uniform and become 'Joe Cool.' It was quite a transformation."

It was that type of transformation that helped Montana lead the Chiefs to a 27-24 overtime playoff win over the Pittsburgh Steelers in his first postseason appearance for his new team.

The Steelers led 17-7 at the half, but Montana rallied the Chiefs with two fourth-quarter touchdowns to knot the score at 24.

Facing a fourth-and-goal from the 7 with 1:48 to play, Montana found receiver Tim Barnett in the back of the end zone to send the game into overtime.

"We're in the huddle," said wide receiver J.J. Birden, who caught a touchdown pass in the first half, "and Joe is calling the play. He looks right at me and smiles and said, 'Don't you just live for this?' Tim Barnett was like the third option on that pass play, and Joe made it look so easy — like he was going to throw the pass to him all along."

Montana was at his best in the big games.

In four Super Bowls, he completed 83 of 122 passes (68 percent) for 1,142 yards with 11 touchdowns and no interceptions. His quarterback rating was 127.8.

Along with the famous Super Bowl "Drive" against Cincinnati, he threw the pass that resulted in "The Catch" by 49ers teammate Dwight Clark. That's when a scrambling Montana lofted the ball in the end zone to Clark. The six-yard touchdown pass, with 51 seconds left, gave the 49ers a 28-27 victory over Dallas for the 1981 NFC championship.

"At his best, when Joe was in sync, he had an intuitive, instinctive nature rarely equaled by any athlete in any sport," Bill Walsh, his San Francisco coach, told ESPN.com.

Montana entered the NFL with a flair for the dramatic. His last collegiate game was at the Cotton Bowl, where he fought off hypothermia to rally the Fighting Irish from a 34-12 deficit to a 35-34 victory. In the 1979 classic, his touchdown pass to Kris Haines as time expired became a part of Notre Dame legend.

Chiefs fans will always remember Montana for that dramatic postseason win over Pittsburgh, the miracle comeback at Denver, and a 24-17 victory over his former 49ers teammates that was witnessed by 79,907 fans in the stands at Arrowhead and more than 400 media in a crowded press box.

"It really wasn't that big of a deal," Montana said, looking back at the game. "It was just the second game (of the 1994 season) and I was playing against some former friends and teammates."

Montana was the only one taking that approach. Chiefs owner Lamar Hunt called it "the game of the century" and former 49ers coach George Seifert said, "Obviously, this is one of the most publicized games and one that stands out a great deal because of all that Joe has done over the years."

While Montana starred on offense, completing 19 of 31 passes for two touchdowns, it was Thomas who stole the show.

The future Hall of Fame linebacker sacked Montana's replacement, Steve Young, three times – including one memorable sack for a safety – and was honored as the NFL Defensive Player of the Week.

"It was a fun afternoon," Thomas said. "We all wanted to win that one for Joe."

Another future Hall of Famer, running back Marcus Allen, was like a rookie after the big win.

"The game was exceptional," said Allen, who carried the ball 20 times for 69 yards and scored on a 4-yard run. "There was a lot of buildup about the match-up between Joe and Steve Young and I think the game lived up to all the hype."

Young enjoyed a solid afternoon, completing 24 of 34 passes for 288 yards, but the teacher came away with a win over the protégé.

"I've learned from the master," Young said, "but we just couldn't get it done today."

On April 18, 1995, in a quiet ceremony inside Arrowhead Stadium, Montana announced his retirement at the age of 38.

He wanted to be able to wrestle and play with his kids and he was concerned that one more year of pounding in the NFL would rob him of those opportunities.

Some of the biggest names in the history of the NFL lauded Montana following his retirement:

"The accomplishments of Joe Montana are a great part of NFL history. When people think of Joe Montana, they think of leadership, of fourth-quarter comebacks and Super Bowl victories. He will always represent the excellence of the NFL," former NFL commissioner Paul Tagliabue said.

"I sincerely believe that Joe was the toughest and most talented quarterback who ever played the game. He was also one of the funniest people I've ever been around. Everybody knows about his ability as a player, but it was his sense of humor that made the package complete," said former 49ers teammate Charles Haley.

"In history, there seems to be great people who come around at a certain time. He was one of those. He came at a time when the game of football was changing. Now they call it the West Coast offense, and he was the perfect man for that kind of offense," former Dallas general manager Tex Schramm said.

"Joe Montana was the greatest quarterback I have ever seen. He did everything that everybody else tried to do and made it look easy. In my 20 years of broadcasting, he was the most dominating player I have ever seen," said Hall of Fame coach and football analyst John Madden.

Montana went on to enjoy a retirement celebration in the Bay Area, because he left his heart in San Francisco.

But Chiefs fans can be so thankful that for two memorable seasons, "Joe Cool's" heart and golden right arm were right here in Kansas City.

# Peterson, Schottenheimer Help Chiefs Escape "The Dark Ages"

*A man left two Chiefs tickets on the dashboard of his car and went into a convenience store. When he returned, there, sitting on his dash, was another pair of tickets.*

Anyone who remained loyal to the Kansas City Chiefs from 1975 to 1988 was a true fan. That period in franchise history was simply known as "the dark ages."

Just ask former Pro Bowl nose tackle Bill Maas, who was the NFL Rookie of the Year in 1984.

"A man left two Chiefs tickets on the dashboard of his car and went into a convenience store to pick up some milk and a loaf of bread," said Maas. "He'd left his window down and thought to himself, 'I hope those tickets are still there when I get back to my car.' When he paid for the items he returned, and there, sitting on his dash, was another pair of tickets."

"Before Marty (Schottenheimer) and Carl (Peterson) came, you couldn't give a Chiefs ticket away. If you asked someone if they wanted a ticket they looked at you like you were crazy."

Chiefs founder and the father of the American Football League, the late Lamar Hunt, wasn't much of a jokester. He was a practical man who saw his team play in the first Super Bowl and win the fourth – giving Kansas City its first world championship.

He suffered through "the dark ages" just like any other fan. As he gazed out the window of his Arrowhead Stadium suite, he saw a bad product on the field and more empty seats than he could count.

In his 14 years with the Chiefs, coach Hank Stram was 124-76-10. After he was fired following a 5-9 record in 1974, the next five Chiefs coaches were a combined 81-128-1, including former special teams coach Frank Gansz, whose 1988 team limped home with four wins.

Hunt shouldered the blame for the Chiefs decline.

"I gave Hank too much responsibility when I made him general manager and director of scouting after we won the Super Bowl," Hunt said. "There was a period when we didn't do a good enough job of scouting and bringing in new players. I blame myself for letting that happen."

Carl Peterson – then the player personnel director of the Philadelphia Eagles – sat in the stands at Arrowhead Stadium midway during Gansz's final season. He wasn't really paying attention to the game. No, he was staring at more than 40,000 empty seats and the team's 1-8 record.

Peterson was an up-and-coming young talent who had played a big role in the resurgence of the Eagles, and Hunt had invited him to Kansas City for his opinion on the team.

Peterson was brutally honest with his future boss, and one day after the 1988 season came to an end, Hunt hired Peterson to be the Chiefs general manager, president and CEO.

Turning the Chiefs around was a daunting task and Peterson knew he had to find the right coach if he ever wanted to lead the Chiefs out of "the dark ages."

The stars must have been aligned for Hunt and Peterson because Marty Schottenheimer, who had come so close to leading the Cleveland Browns to two Super Bowl appearances, only to see those dreams crushed by John Elway and the Denver Broncos, had had a falling out with Browns owner Art Modell and was looking for a change of scenery.

Peterson was a longtime fan of Schottenheimer's and hired him to be the architect of a new plan in Kansas City. Peterson made changes on the field, on the sidelines and in the front office. He wanted to make a game at Arrowhead Stadium an event, but he also knew that the product on the field would play the most important role in the resurrection of a once-proud franchise.

What is the difference between a sofa and a Chiefs fan watching Monday Night Football?

The sofa doesn't keep asking for beer.

"This team has an excellent tradition of winning," Schottenheimer said, "and I don't see why we can't rekindle it."

Added Peterson, "They wanted to sign me to a five-year deal, but I said no. If we can't create a winner here in four years, it's time for someone else to have a shot."

In their first season together, the Chiefs finished with an 8-7-1 record, four wins better than the previous year.

They made linebacker Derrick Thomas their first draft pick and he proved to be the most exciting linebacker to wear the crimson and gold since a couple of guys named Bobby Bell and Willie Lanier.

Peterson brought in veteran players like center Mike Webster, who tutored a kid from Notre Dame named Tim Grunhard, and quarterbacks Ron Jaworski and Steve DeBerg. They gave the team leadership and instant credibility.

New vice-president of administration Tim Connolly sent out a flyer to fans and asked what they missed or what they wanted at the stadium and the overwhelming reply was the return of former bandleader and Kansas City icon Tony DiPardo.

The Chiefs brought back their legendary bandleader, who had stepped away because of illness. He had been with the team since it arrived in Kansas City and the fans welcomed him back with open arms.

The Chiefs cracked down on fan rowdiness, promised a more wholesome and cleaner atmosphere and the end result was a boost in season ticket sales of 23 percent.

Peterson was ying to Schottenheimer's yang. Over a 10-year stretch, they were not only the most successful GM and coach in the league, they were the longest lasting duo in a league that casts aside coaches and front office personnel like yesterday's trash.

While the Marty and Carl Show never achieved the ultimate goal of reaching a Super Bowl, they brought respectability back to One Arrowhead Drive and made it the place to be.

"More than anything else," Peterson said, when asked about the Arrowhead experience, "I love the atmosphere. People plan their tailgating parties weeks in advance and they make a day out of it. Our fans are a big reason for our success and I always want them to be aware of that.

"I think the best thing you can say about Arrowhead Stadium is that opposing teams hate to play here. You can't get a better compliment than that."

Oh, by the way, if you want to crunch some more numbers, no team in the AFC had more fans attend their home games than the Kansas City Chiefs during the 1990s. "The dark ages" were over.

# Vermeil: To "Burnout" and Back

*I'd burned the candle at both ends for so long,*
*I just ran out of gas.*

For many Kansas City Chiefs fans, Dick Vermeil was known as the NFL coach who coined the term "burnout" and left the game, then made a memorable return to lead the St. Louis Rams to their lone world championship.

Not until Vermeil came out of retirement to coach in Kansas City did they realize what a special individual he really was.

"Coach was more like a father to me than a coach," Chiefs kick returner Dante Hall said. "When I was down, he'd pick me up. He and (his wife) Carol mean so much to me. He built up my confidence and was a big reason for my success. He saw something in me that no one else saw. I thanked God every day that he was my coach."

Vermeil coached Pro Bowl quarterback Trent Green in St. Louis, where an injury to Green turned the starting job over to a guy named Kurt Warner, who led the Rams to a Super Bowl triumph.

"Coach Vermeil was a special coach," Green said. "If he believes in you, and he certainly did believe in me, he will work with you to make you a better player. He's a wonderful man and a wonderful coach. I owe him a lot."

That certainly doesn't sound like the man who spent so many hours working while with the Philadelphia Eagles that he stepped away from the game because of burnout.

"The first time around, I'd burned the candle at both ends for so long, I just ran out of gas," Vermeil said. "I really needed a break. When I left, I didn't plan to stay out. I planned to take a year off and then come back into coaching. And they hired me to broadcast, and I enjoyed it. It doubled my salary from what they paid me as football coach at that time, because they didn't pay football coaches very much. I went from $75,000 a year to $150,000 a year – that wasn't too bad – and I was only working 18 weeks."

Despite his success in the broadcast booth, he continued to listen to the coaching offers that poured in.

"I had opportunities for interviews every year but one for 14 years," he said. "I finally decided if I felt good about myself, if I felt back in control of my own work habits and passions to win to the point that if I'm ever going to do it, I better do it now. So when the Rams offered me the job, I took it."

He won a Super Bowl in his third year with the Rams and believed at the time it was the right thing to do to go out on top.

Later, he realized that was a mistake.

"We spent three years building something into the best team in football. It was just the wrong decision to leave."

Today, the smile is quick, and genuine. Vermeil is making the rounds at Arrowhead Stadium visiting family and friends from the organization he coached for five years. He calls receptionists and members of the support staff by their first names. Everyone receives a hug or a slap on the back.

"Oh, gosh, it's great to be back anytime I can make the trip to Kansas City," said Vermeil, who created the most potent offense in the history of the Chiefs, but could not win the team's lone playoff game.

He has retired from coaching, but he hasn't slowed down. He has worked some ESPN football games and gives motivational talks around the country. He does charity work and enjoys being with his family, fishing and working his vineyard in the Napa Valley.

Vermeil has a 126-114 career record in the NFL with stops in Philadelphia (1977-82), St. Louis (1997-99) and Kansas City (2001-05).

Because of his longtime friendship with former Chiefs CEO and president Carl Peterson, Vermeil agreed to return to the coaching ranks after leading the Rams to the Super Bowl.

"When Carl called and asked me to come to the Chiefs, I did it," Vermeil said, matter of factly. "I wasn't interested in any other job or looking for a coaching job, but Carl and I had been together at UCLA and with the Eagles. We were old-time friends. I had broadcast Chiefs games. He'd offered me the job in 1989. It was a good feeling. And I loved (Chiefs owner) Lamar Hunt, so I went.

"And I loved it, I really did."

# Glory Days

The Chiefs played in two of the first four Super Bowls, and vindicated the American Football League with a victory over Minnesota in Super Bowl IV.

This section recalls those "glory days" of the 1960s.

*"M-I-C-K-E-Y M-O-U-S-E . . ."*

# It's Tough to Win a Game When You Carry an Entire League on Your Back

When the American Football League's Kansas City Chiefs braced to meet the Green Bay Packers – the NFL version of royalty – in the first Super Bowl, Chiefs quarterback Len Dawson was consumed by the Mickey Mouse theme song.

"M-I-C-K-E-Y M-O-U-S-E . . ."

Huh?

"All the talk surrounding the game centered on the Packers and how they were the superior team and the superior league," Dawson said. "We weren't just playing for our team and our city, we were playing for an entire league.

"They were the older, more experienced league, but we had some pretty good teams in the AFL and we had some pretty darned good players play in that game. But not everyone thought that way."

*We went into that game carrying the entire AFL on our back.*

Even though Walt Disney created Mickey Mouse in a downtown Kansas City studio, Dawson and his Chiefs teammates wanted nothing to do with the famous animated rodent.

It had nothing to do with his cartoon antics. No, it had more to do with some comments made about the American Football League by *Sports Illustrated's* national football writer, Tex Maule, who called the AFL a "Mickey Mouse league" in a conversation following a Green Bay Packers game.

"We went into that game carrying the entire AFL on our back," Dawson said. "Looking back on it, we were extremely confident going into the championship game against the Bills (a 31-3 AFL championship victory that led to the Super Bowl), but we weren't that confident going into the game against the Packers.

"We were a young team. I was one of the oldest guys on the team, and we had the talent to play with them, but on that sunny day in Los Angeles, they were the better team."

Chiefs coach Hank Stram recalled the heated AFL-NFL debate leading up to that game.

"There was a war of words," Stram said. "We were all eager to get it settled on the field. There was all the intrigue and drama of the early years, with the AFL and NFL going after the star collegiate players. We were lucky enough to win the AFL championship and represent our league in the first Super Bowl, and when we lost that game it was a professional blow. Our organization didn't lose, the entire league lost. And we felt that and it was tough to deal with. They were calling us the Mickey Mouse League and those comments hurt."

So Stram issued a gag order for his team: No bad-mouthing the Packers or the NFL.

"Hank didn't want any trouble," said Fred "The Hammer" Williamson, a defensive back who went on to enjoy a successful career in Hollywood where he appeared in several movies.

"I wanted to get the attention focused on me, to take the pressure off the other guys."

Williamson talked about how he was going to lay the hammer down on the Packers, which provided good bulletin board material for the 13-point favorites.

"I don't think Fred did us a favor by saying all the things he did," Dawson said, "but at least he was confident going into the game."

The first Super Bowl wasn't quite the extravaganza it is today. There were 338 print media and 262 electronic media credentials issued. (By contrast, there were more than 13,000 credentials issued from all over the globe to Super Bowl XLI in Miami in 2007.) A "spaceman" wearing a jet pack – similar to one that was featured in a James Bond film – thrilled the first Super Bowl crowd of 61,000 fans, who somehow seemed lost in the 90,000-seat Los Angeles Coliseum. Tickets were $10 and $12. Face value tickets to the latest Super Bowl were $600 and $700 and many were sold via ticket booking agencies for five to 10 times that amount.

"Lamar Hunt always thought the Super Bowl was going to be big," Dawson said, "but I don't think anyone thought it would be what it is today. It's almost as if the game can get lost in everything that goes on during the week of the game. All the Hall of Fame guys are down there, there are more parties than you can count, and look at the entertainment. We had a guy fly around the stadium and a couple of bands."

Prince, the Rolling Stones, Paul McCartney, Tom Petty and Bruce Springsteen have performed at recent Super Bowls, and Janet Jackson's revealing performance from a few years back will be remembered long after the winner of this year's event is forgotten about.

Packers coach Vince Lombardi would have nothing to do with all the hype surrounding the first Super Bowl. He took his team 90 miles up the coast of California and practiced away from all the scrutiny.

"Our plan was to get inside (defensive back Willie) Mitchell," Lombardi said. "They were daring us to pass. That stacked defense worked well against the run, but we felt like we could get inside Mitchell and he wouldn't have any help."

Lombardi had the perfect quarterback to execute that plan in Bart Starr, an accurate passer who never put up huge numbers because he was basically asked to hand the ball off to running backs Jim Taylor and Paul Hornung.

"Our game plan was perfect," Starr said. "We knew exactly what we wanted to do, and they had a hard time stopping it."

Wide receiver Max McGee emerged as a hero for the Packers, and he happened to have been out on the town the night before the big game because he didn't think he would see any action. McGee was an 11-year veteran backup to wide receiver Boyd Dowler.

Although McGee never verified this, legend has it that he returned to his hotel room at 7 a.m. the day of the Super Bowl. When Dowler was injured early in the game, McGee went in, caught seven passes for 138 yards, and scored two touchdowns. He scored the first touchdown in Super Bowl history when he reached out with one arm and somehow managed to snag a pass that had been tipped by Mitchell. He rumbled 37 yards for the score and the Packers led 7-0.

The play didn't rattle the Chiefs as Dawson hit Otis Taylor on a 31-yard pass play that put the ball on the Packers 7. On the next play, running backs Curtis McClinton and Bert Coan were both standing alone in the end zone and Dawson fired a perfect strike to McClinton to knot the score.

Jim Taylor then scored on a 14-yard run for the Packers and the Chiefs got a 31-yard field goal from Mike Mercer to make the halftime score 14-10 in favor of the Packers.

"We were confident at the half," the Chiefs' Bobby Bell said. "We all felt like we had played well, stuck to the game plan and that we could come out and make something big happen in the second half."

Something big did happen in the second half, and to this day it causes nightmares for Dawson.

Facing a Packers blitz, Dawson looked for tight end Fred Arbanas on the right side of the field. His off-balance pass was tipped and intercepted by Willie Wood on the Chiefs' 45.

> What's the difference between a Raiders fan and a chimp?
>
> One is hairy, stupid, and smells, and the other is a chimp.

Wood returned it to the Chiefs' 5 and Elijah Pitts scored on the next play and suddenly, the Packers had momentum and a 21-10 lead.

"If there is one play I could have back in my entire career," Dawson said, "it would be that one pass."

Although he never pointed an accusing finger at Dawson, Stram said, "I would like to think that one play doesn't make a difference in an entire game, but in that case it did. Our personality changed; we diverted from our game plan."

Offensive lineman Dave Hill recalls, "After they got the big lead, they started coming after Lenny. They were throwing everything at us, and we didn't do a very good job of stopping them."

Dawson and backup Pete Beathard were sacked five times in the second half.

McGee caught a 13-yard touchdown pass, Pitts scored on a 1-yard run and the Packers proved the world right by claiming a convincing victory over the Chiefs.

"You have to give Green Bay a lot of credit," said former Chiefs general manager Jack Steadman. "They had everything to lose and we had everything to gain. Lombardi was getting a lot of pressure."

Arbanas still wonders what might have happened if the ball had not been tipped.

"I was open and could have had some running room," the all-time AFL tight end said. "They caught us off guard with that blitz."

Dawson agrees.

"They hadn't blitzed the entire game. I made the biggest mistake a quarterback can make – just take a loss and don't turn the ball over. I've replayed that pass over and over and over again in my mind."

And if you're wondering what happened to "The Hammer," he was knocked unconscious by Packers running back Donny Anderson early in the game and never returned to action.

After the game, Lombardi received the championship trophy – which today bears his name – and said, "Kansas City has a good team. But it doesn't compare with some of the top teams in the NFL."

The Chiefs bristled at those comments and vowed to return to Super Bowl action to prove they belonged with the elite teams in pro football.

*"M-I-C-K-E-Y M-O-U-S-E . . .*
*Mickey Mouse, Mickey Mouse, forever let us hold our*
*banner*
*High! High! High! High!*
*Come along and sing a song*
*And join the jamboree!*
*M-I-C-K-E-Y M-O-U-S-E!"*

Three years later, that song would become a distant memory as the Chiefs held the banner high, high, high as the last American Football League team to win a Super Bowl, upsetting Minnesota 23-7 in Super Bowl IV.

# 'Bell Had No Business Being There'

*Most Chiefs fans remember the team's victory in Super Bowl IV, but few can recall the road to the ultimate victory. The Chiefs had to fight past the New York Jets, with their star quarterback Joe Namath, and the hated Oakland Raiders in the playoffs. This series of stories recounts the playoff games, and the Super Bowl victory.*

Bobby Bell bit his lower lip, wiped some grit and grime from his eyes, and glanced at the scoreboard.

"We were leading 6-3," the Chiefs Hall of Fame linebacker said, "and we knew we had to come up with the defensive stand of our lives. If we didn't, we were heading home – and none of us wanted that to happen."

"Broadway" Joe Namath led his Jets to the 1-yard line, as the wind swirled and howled through Shea Stadium in New York. The year before, Namath had led the Jets to one of the biggest upsets in pro football history, stunning the heavily favored Baltimore Colts in Super Bowl III. Now, he was a yard away from taking a late lead against the Chiefs.

"Our defensive stand in that game," Chiefs Hall of Fame linebacker Willie Lanier said, "was inspirational. It was the most significant single defensive series I was ever a part of."

Chiefs defensive lineman Jerry Mays said at the time, "It was something that doesn't happen in 10 or 20 years. We were high; it was indescribable. The defensive unit had played well the entire game, then Willie got us. He fired me up. It was the way he did it – tears in his eyes, teeth gnashing."

> *Otis knelt down on the sidelines and actually
> diagramed this play in the turf.*

While the defense was frustrating Namath and Co., Chiefs wide receiver Otis Taylor approached Len Dawson about a possible pass play.

"There were times our receivers would come up to me on the sidelines and talk about a possible play," Dawson said. "Otis knelt down on the sidelines and actually diagramed this play in the turf.

"He said the free safety can't guard me and he came up with this play and I thought, 'That can work.' As we went out to the field on our next series, Otis came up to me and said, 'Think you'll call the play?' Well, with my sense of humor I replied, 'No, not until we get in the huddle.'

"The play Otis came up with worked to perfection. Now, you have to understand that the wind was blowing and it was cold and miserable and Joe was having a hard time getting his passes to do what he wanted them to do. A lot of the passes he was throwing were just dying out there, getting knocked down by the wind.

"I knew I needed a good release and a good spiral and I let the ball go. At first, I thought I'd thrown it too far, but thank goodness Otis has a different gear and he catches up with the ball and it goes for about a 61-yard gain."

Dawson hit Gloster Richardson for the game-winning touchdown pass on the next play.

# Packing Their Bags for the Super Bowl

The Chiefs desperately wanted to get back to the Super Bowl. They had been humiliated by the Green Bay Packers in Super Bowl I. NFL fans and players went so far as to call them members of a "Mickey Mouse league," a derisive reference to the underdog American Football League.

But to get to New Orleans, the site of Super Bowl IV, the Chiefs had to accomplish something they had not come close to doing during the regular season – beat the Oakland Raiders.

"We hated the Raiders and they hated us," Hall of Fame linebacker Bobby Bell said. "They had our number back then, and we knew we had to play a perfect game to get a win and go on to the Super Bowl."

The Raiders had defeated the Chiefs 41-6 in a special playoff game following a regular season in which both teams had finished with 12-2 records. That loss forced the Chiefs to travel to New York, where they turned in the defensive series of the season to frustrate the Jets and Joe Namath.

Chiefs coach Hank Stram wanted the same type of intensity from his team, so he had the team practice in black and silver jerseys – the team colors of the hated Raiders. Because the Super Bowl was going to be played in New Orleans, the Raiders feasted on Cajun food with a Mardi Gras theme before their playoff encounter with the Chiefs.

"Hank was really mad," Bell said, "and it fired the rest of us up. Not that we really needed to be fired up to play the Raiders."

The Raiders took a quick 7-0 lead on a 3-yard run by Charlie Smith.

"Although the Raiders had dominated us for the past three seasons and the first half of that game," Len Dawson said, "there was no panic on our part. We trailed 7-0 but felt like something good was going to happen."

Early in the second half, Dawson hit Frank Pitts in the flat and the big wide receiver muscled his way to the Raiders 1. Fullback Wendell Hayes ran for a touchdown, which knotted the score at 7-7. Raiders quarterback Daryle Lamonica then struck his hand on the helmet of Chiefs defensive end Aaron Brown on a pass attempt and eventually had to turn the offense over to veteran quarterback and Chiefs killer George Blanda.

With the ball on the Kansas City 24, Blanda saw Warren Wells alone near the 5-yard line. He threw a tight spiral, but Wells slipped and the ball was intercepted by Emmitt Thomas in the end zone. He returned it to the 6.

"We had a play where Otis Taylor lined up between the guard and tackle and took off towards the sideline," Dawson said. "I called Otis' number and threw the ball so only he could catch it – which he did."

Five plays later, Robert Holmes scored and the Chiefs had a 14-7 lead.

"The way our defense was playing," Dawson said, "we felt pretty confident. But we wanted to put more points on the scoreboard."

The Chiefs survived three fourth-quarter fumbles and Thomas came up with his second interception, setting up a 22-yard field goal by Jan Stenerud. The Chiefs had an improbable 17-7 victory.

"In back-to-back weeks, our defense held Joe Namath and the Jets to two field goals and the Raiders to one touchdown," Dawson said. "I think that is too often overlooked."

After the game, Stram stood by the Chiefs bus and motioned to Bell, who had just exited the stadium.

"Coach pointed over to some Raiders," Bell said. "They were carrying their suitcases home. They thought they were going to New Orleans. But all they were doing was going home."

## This One Was Really Super!

The backgrounds of Len Dawson and Jan Stenerud are about as varied as their path to superstardom in the NFL.

Dawson grew up in Alliance, Ohio – in the shadows of what is now the Pro Football Hall of Fame. Stenerud was born in Fetsund, Norway, and dreamed of making his country's Olympic ski jumping team.

While he was a teenager in Norway, Stenerud had no idea what professional football was all about, while

Dawson hoped that one day he might play in the National Football League.

Because of the innovative mind of Kansas City Chiefs head coach Hank Stram, who rescued Dawson off the NFL's scrap heap and later took a chance on a lanky ski jumper who had a knack for kicking the football, Dawson and Stenerud teamed up to lead the Chiefs to their only world championship.

It all took place in Super Bowl IV, where Stenerud starred with his leg and Dawson overcame a brutal week of off-field scrutiny to turn in an MVP performance, leading the Chiefs to a 23-7 victory over the heavily favored Minnesota Vikings.

Stenerud got the Chiefs on the scoreboard with a then-Super Bowl record 48-yard field goal. He followed with 32- and 25-yard kicks. Mike Garrett scored on a short run to give the Chiefs a 16-0 lead going into the halftime locker room.

"At halftime, we had the lead," Stenerud said, "and we're half an hour away from the world championship. And because of all the halftime activities, it lasted twice as long as a normal halftime. It seemed 10 times as long. I remember that clearly, and how strange that was. We had the momentum going, but when we went out there, it was almost like starting a new game."

*If your name was associated with gambling, that was like the kiss of death.*

Dawson, who was the victim of a bogus gambling probe the week before the biggest game of his life, had hoped to avoid any pre-game distractions.

"You've got that right," chuckled Dawson, the MVP of Super Bowl IV. "You especially want to avoid the type of distractions that come from the nightly news."

A national newscast reported that Dawson was one of several NFL players, including Namath, who were going to have to testify before a grand jury in Detroit as part of a gambling investigation.

"Now, I've been blindsided in my day, but never like that," said Dawson, who professed his innocence. "And I wasn't the only one named. We were supposed to get subpoenas in 10 days. But I never did get one. Today, all the talk is about steroids and cheating in sports. Back then, if your name was associated with gambling, that was like the kiss of death."

Dawson's name had been found in the directory of known gambler Donald Dawson (no relation), who had $400,000 in checks and cashier's checks when he was arrested.

"He had my number and a lot of players' numbers," Dawson said. "I'd met him when I played for Pittsburgh. That was 10 years ago. When I hurt my knee (during the 1969 season that led up to Super Bowl IV) he called me. When my father passed away that same season, he called again. That was it. Now, this big investigation is going on and everyone is asking me what I want to do. I told everyone the truth. I knew the guy. I wasn't going to make matters worse by saying I didn't know him."

Stram invited Dawson to take over his suite in the Fountainbleau Hotel in New Orleans so he could avoid all the late-night phone calls and the media crush.

"I don't think Johnny (Robinson, Dawson's roommate) has ever forgiven me," Dawson said, grinning. "He got calls around the clock – and they were all for me."

Dawson met with team owner Lamar Hunt, Stram and team officials and came up with the following statement (*reprinted courtesy of the Kansas City Chiefs*):

"My name has been mentioned in regard to an investigation conducted by the Justice Department. I have not been contacted by any law enforcement agency or apprised of any reason why my name has been brought up. The only reason I can think of is that I have a casual acquaintance with Mr. Donald Dawson of Detroit, who I understand has been charged in the investigation. Mr. Dawson is not a relative of mine. I have known Mr. Dawson for about 10 years and have talked with him on several occasions. My only conversations with him in recent years concerned my knee injury and the death of my father. On these occasions he called me to offer his sympathy. These calls were among the many I received. Gentlemen, this is all I have to say. I have told you everything I know."

The next morning, Dawson read the same statement in front of his teammates. When he was done, the coach asked if there were any questions.

"Yeah, have our tickets come in yet?" asked center E.J. Holub.

Dawson simply smiled. He knew he had the support of his team, and that was all that mattered.

"What happened to Lenny made us mad," linebacker Bobby Bell said, "and fired us up. I think it might have helped us come together as a team."

Dawson was at his best against the Vikings. He ran the Chiefs offense with the precision of a surgeon.

Minnesota finally got on the scoreboard in the third quarter when Dave Osborn scored on a 4-yard run, but all that did was set the stage for the biggest touchdown in Otis Taylor's brilliant career.

It was a pass from Dawson to Taylor, who caught the ball in the right flat.

"I threw the pass, but Otis did all the work," Dawson said.

Taylor ran down the sidelines – sidestepping one defender, then stiff-arming another near the 10-yard line – to make the score 23-7.

"It's a play I will never forget," Taylor said at a Chiefs' Super Bowl anniversary reception. "The defense had done such a great job getting us to the Super Bowl. I was so honored to contribute to that win. A lot of fans in Kansas City still remember that touchdown."

If you see an Oakland Raiders fan on a bike, why should you not swerve to hit him?

It could be your bike.

The Chiefs have honored the play with a large diorama that features the high-stepping Taylor striding into the end zone. The large display piece will find a home in the new Arrowhead Stadium Chiefs Hall of Fame.

"It was just a great feeling to be in a winning locker room," said Dawson, who received a congratulatory phone call from then-President Richard Nixon after the game. "That was the last time an AFL team would ever play an NFL team because of the merger and we came out on top."

Stenerud didn't talk to the king of Norway in the noisy locker room, but that didn't take away from his post-game memories.

"I remember the total elation when the game was over," Stenerud said. "I am not one to scream and yell. But it was a terrific feeling of accomplishment. And I also remember thinking about the other guys who had played for so long in the AFL. To beat the old league in the last game between the two leagues, I know how terrific it felt for them."

# Home of the Best Fans in the NFL

Neither rain nor snow nor the darkest of seasons can keep Chiefs' fans from loving their team.

From Old Municipal Stadium to Arrowhead ... wherever the Chiefs call home, the best fans in the NFL are there!

*"If there would have been a roof on Arrowhead, it would have exploded."*

# It's a Jungle Out There – Dress Appropriately

Photo courtesy of Scott E. Thomas Photography

Former Kansas City Chiefs wide receiver Andre Rison would strike a Spiderman pose following each of his touchdown receptions in the late 1990s.

While the controversial former star slipped into his comic book character persona during the game, Monte Short is Arrowman 24 hours a day.

If you've ever seen a Chiefs game in person or on television, picked up a piece of literature about the Chiefs, or read about them in a national publication like *Athlon's Football*, you've seen Short ... oops, Arrowman.

Make that Hall of Famer Arrowman. He was selected from thousands of entries to represent the Kansas City Chiefs in a special fans-only exhibit at the Pro Football Hall of Fame in Canton, Ohio.

Not bad for a guy who's stuck up – with arrows, that is.

He dreamed up the idea back in 1992 so that a friend would keep asking him to his spectacular tailgate parties.

"My buddy Todd Walters had these great tailgate parties and I went to one dressed up for the Chiefs game," said Short. "They really made a big deal out of my outfit, so I decided to really do something special."

Arrowman was born.

Today's version is a sleek, highly stylized arrow-clad outfit compared to the old days. It might feature a hated Chiefs opponent or even a referee. No one escapes Short's wit and artistic flair.

"Let me tell you," Short said, with a grin, "when I first started doing this, I was trying to find different ways to get the arrows to stay put."

He went to a sporting goods store, bought some real arrows and stuck them in a board underneath his shirt.

"Bad idea," he said with a laugh, "I had to come up with something better."

Over the past six years, he has devised an Arrowman outfit that poses no danger to Short or to the folks sitting around him at Arrowhead Stadium. It features rubber tubing with homemade arrowheads, all adorned with Chiefs logos.

His two favorite outfits, which take up to 12 hours to make, are a No. 7 Denver jersey and a No. 0 Raiders jersey.

The No. 7 is John Elway's number and No. 0 represents the hated owner of the men in silver and black, Al Davis.

Short enjoyed a visit with a special friend when he attended a Dallas Cowboys game in Irving, Texas, a few years back.

"I was in the stands having a good time with all the Cowboy fans when someone came up to me and taps me on the back," Short said. "I turned around and it was (Chiefs owner) Lamar Hunt.

"He'd seen me from his suite in the stadium and came down to talk to me. I couldn't believe it."

Unlike many modern-day Chiefs fans, who jumped on the team's bandwagon when coach Marty Schottenheimer came on board in 1989, Short was a Chiefs fan back when they won their first Super Bowl.

In fact, that victory got him kicked out of Van Horn High School for a day.

"I wanted to skip school and go to the parade in downtown Kansas City," Short said, "so I told the nurse I was sick. She didn't believe me. She told me I was going to the parade.

"Well, she was right. But I ran out of her office and all the time while I was at the parade I was afraid the cops were going to arrest me."

He was suspended from school for one day, but said it was all worth it.

So has all the work and hours he's put into his elaborate Arrowman costumes.

He is one of just 31 fans who will be inducted into their own special branch of the Hall of Fame in Canton, Ohio.

Short has a thick scrapbook that has documented most of his exploits in national publications across the country. There are even a few clips from his hometown paper, *The Independence Examiner.*

"I'll tell you something," he said, "*The Examiner* will always be special for me. My first job was delivering *The Examiner*."

From paperboy to Arrowman to Canton – only in America.

# A Super Fan with a Heart

Like most Americans, Monte Short was devastated when he heard about the terrorist attacks in New York City and Washington, D.C., on Sept. 11, 2001

Short reached into his pocket and made contributions to many relief efforts, but he reached into his soul and made a difference for one special burn victim.

When Short, who is best known as "Arrowman" – the first fan from Kansas City to be inducted into the Pro Football Hall of Fame – heard about a soldier who was burned over 60 percent of his body in the Pentagon attack, he went to work.

Army Lt. Col. Brian Birdwell is a native of Texas, but while stationed at Fort Riley and Fort Leavenworth in Kansas, he became a big Kansas City Chiefs fan.

"I guess he was a tailgater and everything," Short said. "I heard he was in very bad shape and that the upper part of his body was burned pretty bad."

When Short heard of Birdwell's condition, he thought about making a huge greeting card and having someone from the Chiefs organization take it to Washington before a game against the Redskins.

"But then I thought, 'How can you get a big card on a plane?' Then I began to think about a banner."

Short and his wife, Stacie, began work on a gigantic red and gold banner that began in three pieces.

Short took the banner to several area locations. "I don't even want to guess how many people signed it," Short said, "but there are a lot of signatures on there."

Short talked to Chiefs officials, and the banner and its messages found their way to the burn unit of Washington Hospital Burn Center.

"For most of us, it's easy to give a couple of bucks to the relief effort," Short said, "but I wanted to do something more personal.

"And the response to this banner has been amazing."

Birdwell received more than two mail bags of cards and packages from the Kansas City area.

"The hospital staff told my wife that there was too much for them to keep at the hospital," Short said. "They had to take it to his home."

"We've seen a lot of good things happen since that day (of the attack) and it really does make you proud to be an American."

# Brian Birdwell: A Fan Who Will Always Be a Part of the Chiefs Family

*Brian Birdwell is like most Chiefs fans. He has a passion for the team and would do anything he could to help it advance in the playoffs. Also, like most Chiefs fans, if Birdwell's not watching the Chiefs in person – which he's done not only at Arrowhead but also at other stadiums –*

*he's wearing his Chiefs garb and watching or listening with family and friends. But that's about where the similarities between Birdwell and other Chiefs fans end. Birdwell, who's originally from Texas, made the Army his career. He was stationed at Fort Riley during the summer of 1983 and 1986-89, and at Fort Leavenworth during 1993-97 and 1999-2000. On the morning of September 11, 2001, Birdwell was in his office at the Pentagon when terrorists crashed American Flight 77 into the building. Birdwell, who suffered second- and third-degree burns over 60 percent of his body, spent 12 weeks in the hospital but he miraculously survived. He and his wife Mel and their son Matthew learned during that time (and since) what it means to be a part of the Chiefs family.*

"We were invited to Kansas City for the home opener in 2002 against Jacksonville to do the coin toss. The honor of tossing the coin, to me, was a great opportunity to represent the Armed Forces. I wasn't just representing Chiefs fans who are in the military, scattered around the world, but other service men and women who aren't necessarily Chiefs fans. But the Chiefs do a great job of honoring men and women in the military. To me, this day was an opportunity for American service men and women to say thank you to some great citizens who happened to be wearing red that day. People in the Kansas City region understand the fight that we're in. This war isn't only about Americans. It's about a culture of depravity and death that believes it rational to fly planes into buildings, or drive trucks laden with bombs into buildings, or strap bombs on their young children and walk them into crowds. Fighting that type of enemy, you can defend every port and every piece of critical territory in this nation and you've done nothing but change your enemy's target set. You have done nothing to impose your will upon them. The only way to defeat it is to go change that culture. The people of the Kansas City area understand that and they appreciate that. It's nice to know that the people of Kansas City weren't just saying, 'Thanks for being a Chiefs fan.' They were acknowledging the sacrifice of our service men and women. The Chiefs have always championed those who put on the uniform. The Chiefs recognize that they are in the entertainment business, but that the service men and women are not in entertainment. They understand that value, which is very telling of the Chiefs organization. I was given a neat opportunity to express thanks to the Chiefs and their fans for that understanding and appreciation.

When I got the letter in July, asking if I'd go to Kansas City to do that, it was a no brainer. Although the Chiefs invited Mel and me, we also wanted to bring our son Matt and one of our friends, Dennis Boykin, who is a huge Chiefs fan. But also, Dennis and his wife Joyce took care of our dog while I was in the hospital for three months after the September 11 attacks. (It takes someone very special to take care of your child. It also takes special people to take care of your dog.) We offered to take care of the hotel and travel for Dennis and Matt. The Chiefs arranged for two extra seats very graciously, so we could bring them.

I'm not sure how this happened, but somewhere between 1999 and 2002, Matt somehow became a Jacksonville fan. I don't know if he really liked the

Jaguars or he just couldn't like my team. But somewhere in those three years I went wrong with him. When Mel and I first talked about the letter, we asked Matt if he wanted to go. We told him it'd be in Kansas City in September and that I'd get to toss the coin. He wasn't too thrilled about going. When I told him they were playing the Jaguars, however, he about jumped out of his seat for the chance. Of course, since I was going to be wearing the jersey that the Chiefs had given me, Matt said he was going to wear his Mark Brunell (then the Jacksonville quarterback) jersey.

Sure enough, on game day, Matt was sitting there on the front row of Lamar Hunt's/Carl Peterson's suite, actively cheering for the Jaguars. We were giving him looks like, "We're going to throw you over this balcony if you don't watch it." As the game was drawing to a close and Jacksonville was obviously going to win, Mr. Hunt told Matt: "I have to hand it to you, kid. You've got a lot of guts to come into my booth and root for the other team." I don't know if Matt was proud of that, but he certainly wasn't ashamed of it.

During the game, I went on the radio with Mitch Holthus and Len Dawson. One of the best things I was able to tell them was thanks to the Chiefs for starting to stream the games on the Web site, because it allowed men and women in the Armed Forces to listen to them from around the world. There are a lot of friends of mine in the service who like to listen to games.

It was important that they streamed those games because there are guys on aircraft flying over the Indian Ocean or ships out at sea or other service men and women on land in the Marines Corps or in the Army, who listen to the Chiefs games. A friend of mine, Brian Leekey, who was in Saudi Arabia for 18 months as an advisor to the Saudi army, would listen to the Chiefs games. (So, of course, I told him hello on the radio during the Jacksonville game.) Armed Forces Network is over there, but you only get whatever the national game is. So, of the 13 games on Sunday, you get the biggest national draw. If it didn't have Kansas City, or if the Chiefs weren't playing on Sunday night or Monday night, we wouldn't hear them. It was important that Mitch and Len knew that they not only have great listeners in Kansas City and other places on their network, but also a whole cadre of military personnel around the world listening.

Two stories that come to mind center around that. When I was stationed at Fort Lewis, Washington, I was on the First Corps of Staff in the G-4; I'm a logistics officer by trade (now retired). All of First Corps has the Pacific Rim regional responsibility, so we do a lot of interaction with Thailand, Japan, South Korea and sometimes Australia. About three months after I arrived at Fort Lewis, a group of us traveled to Tokyo for a planning conference for a week with the Japanese Ground Self-Defense Forces. I knew Brian Leekey, but I didn't know he was a Chiefs fan at the time. I was sitting across from him when he got out his laptop computer to start putting together the mission analysis that we were going to do. When he turned on the laptop, the screensaver was the one that the Chiefs put out in 1995, when they went 13-3. (I also happened to have that on my home computer.) When that popped up and started playing "Go Chiefs," I excitedly said something to him. It's kind of like when two Texans meet each other in another part of the country. Here we are in this conference room dungeon, in a basement of an old building in Camp Zama, Japan, having a Chiefs moment in July 1997. We reminisced about the great moments and all the games that broke our hearts. Of course, the 1995 season was a heartbreaker and in '96 we didn't make the playoffs.

One of the best things about being at Fort Lewis in Seattle at that time was that the Seahawks were in the Chiefs division, so we knew the Chiefs were going to be in town once during the season. Luckily, Seattle also was the easiest city in the division to get tickets because the team hadn't been good for so long. So in July in Japan, Brian and I started to plot our trip to the game. Brian knew a couple folks who were Chiefs fans and I knew a couple folks who were Chiefs fans, and we started getting the word out that we were going to the Chiefs-Seahawks game, which was going to be in November. We bought tickets for 33 Chiefs fans from Fort Lewis to go to the game that day. We had folks scattered from all over Fort Lewis attending that game. (On a side note, Dennis Boykin, who went to the Jacksonville game at Arrowhead in 2002, was stationed at Leavenworth in 1997, and he and his wife Joyce flew out to Seattle for this Chiefs game. Dennis and I had been in some of the same units or on some of the same installations for 14 years, which is highly unlikely.) I went and bought all of the tickets at one time so

What's the difference between a winning Raiders team and a UFO?

Someone has seen a UFO.

we could sit in the same area. We were in the upper deck of the Kingdome, a big square of red. Then there were smaller pockets of Chiefs fans scattered throughout the stadium. Much like some of the Chiefs ultimate fans like Belly Boy or Arrowman, the Seahawks had a fan like that, who wasn't on the field but he was the ultimate Seahawks fanatic. His body was painted blue and sea foam green and he was wearing an Uncle Sam-type top hat painted green. He was so impressed with our group of Chiefs fans that he came up to the upper deck to talk to us personally. Really, all the Seahawk fans were very courteous. When Dennis and I were in Baltimore during the 2003 season, we were sitting next to Ravens fans, and there was some pretty good banter going back and forth. But in Seattle, as long as a Seahawks fan has his latte in hand, there's never any violence. The Chiefs won the game behind Rich Gannon, playing for an injured Elvis Grbac.

As usual, it was pouring rain that day, so we were standing partially under cover, partially in the rain, watching the team busses load. While we were waiting for the team to come out, we started talking with a Seattle police officer. Two weeks before, the Seahawks' home game had been against the Raiders. We told him about how we'd go to about any away game, except Oakland. Brian and I always joke about how the NFL sanctions all the games during the season except the two games between the Raiders and the Chiefs. The league lets the Federal Bureau of Prisons sanction those. It's a prison riot in Oakland with cheerleaders. If I remember correctly, during my years at Leavenworth, 1993-97, Don

Fortune, on his radio show, gave away tickets to Chiefs road games, except the Raiders game. They would not give away tickets to the Raiders game because it was that unhealthy. The only other stadium that's close to that would be Philadelphia. A couple of years ago, the city brought in a municipal judge so that as the police were arresting people for being drunk or fighting, they would be carted away. That way, instead of the people being back the next week, they would be taken to the court immediately and would sentence guys to 60 or 90 days, and they'd lose season tickets. It was getting so unruly.

I'm convinced, though, that the entire Chiefs family, from Mr. Hunt all the way to the newest fan, is one of the best and classiest in the NFL. While I was in the hospital after the September 11 attacks, I received a couple special visitors.

One was former Chiefs kicker Nick Lowery, who came to the hospital twice and later came to our house. I remember pieces of Nick Lowery's second visit, but not his first. At the time of the first, he was a student at Harvard's Institute of Public Affairs and his parents live in the Washington, D.C. area. There are photographs of that first visit, but I don't recall that one because of all the medication the doctors had me on. The next time Nick visited was the day before I got out of intensive care. That, and a visit he made to our house, is when I realized how big he really is ... 6'5", 210 pounds or so. Not a small man. You always think of kickers as dweeby kind of guys, but Nick's one of the biggest fellas I've ever met. Compared to the linemen, Nick's small but not so next to people I know. The second time he came to the hospital, he brought a football that he had kicked in 1980 for his first game-winning field goal in a Chiefs win over the Lions. The Chiefs won 20-17. As with many commemorative footballs, they took out a panel of the ball and put a special panel on it. That new panel has the date and details of the game, and then Nick signed it. I'm proud of that football, which is now mounted in a display in our home.

Nick later came to visit us at the house. I had received a jersey from the Chiefs with my name on it, which I still have. I wore it to the Colts playoff game and also the game against Jacksonville. I mentioned to Nick that short of Lamar Hunt and Carl Peterson, I didn't know who to thank for that. Nick knew who, so he called Mike Davidson, the equipment manager, from our house and I thanked him for the jersey. (I got to meet Mike on the sideline at the Jacksonville game in Jacksonville, so I thanked him again. That was a great experience.) When I was a kid, I was a kicker because that's about the only part of football I could practice by myself. So, having Nick Lowery, one of the greatest Chiefs kickers of all time, visit me at the hospital and then at my house was pretty neat.

Following the September 11 attacks, Chiefs fans have shown what it means to be part of this great family.

In May of 2000, Mr. Hunt opened Arrowhead for the first public practice there. Fans could come out and watch drills. Brian Leekey, his boys, Matt and I went to that. That was absolutely the right thing to do for any Chiefs fan. In Washington, when Daniel Snyder first took over the Redskins, he opened up practice but he charged something like $15 for parking and then something for tickets. It wasn't done right. The one with the Chiefs was done right because admission was free and a very nominal fee for parking. Monte Short, aka Arrowman, was running through the crowd, giving away cards. Just as the practice was over, he was in our area and gave away a card that he had signed, "Arrowman." Under the glass on my desk at the office in the Pentagon, I had his card. Being the rabid Chiefs fan that I am, also in my office before September 11 was an action figure of Len Dawson, a mini Chiefs helmet and a couple of other pieces of Chiefs memorabilia. The morning of the attack, all of those things burned. The Chiefs fans overwhelmingly replaced all those things and more.

The Sunday before the attack, I was at Dennis' house watching the Chiefs-Raiders, which went into overtime. When I got out of the hospital and the hospital's hotel 12 weeks later, the first game I was able to watch was Chiefs-Raiders, the second time they played that season. This also was the first time I was going to see my dog in more than 12 weeks. This was on the 13th of December. We went to Dennis' house, watched the game and it almost went into overtime. Dennis and I were sitting there looking at each other right before the kick, I said, "Dennis, the last game I was at your house and the Chiefs-Raiders game went into overtime, something very horrific happened in my life on the following Tuesday. If this game goes into overtime and something horrific happens on Tuesday, I'm never coming back to your house." So there was somewhat of a relief when the Chiefs lost in regulation. Brian and I were at the Chiefs-Raiders game on January 2, 2000. Had we won that game, we would have been 10-6 and won the AFC West. Instead, we lost, went 9-7 and got bumped from the playoffs. We've shared those heartbreaking moments even if we haven't been in Kansas City. There also have been a lot of great moments as a Chiefs fan. Like every Chiefs fan, I feel the pain of the losses and the exhilaration of the good times.

The desire for victory is so intense, that all of us as fans would do whatever we could to see it happen. At the playoff game against the Colts, Brian and I had the opportunity to go to the tent of 101 the Fox, and meet some of the folks from the radio network. One of the guys asked me how I thought the Chiefs would do that day. Brian jumped in and said, "Oh, man, we're going to win!" I went on and gave my description of how I expected the Chiefs to win.

I can't imagine not being a Chiefs fan. I've put far too much rigor into the team. Our entire downstairs basement is done in a Chiefs motif from the football signed by Coach Dick Vermeil and the helmet signed by the team, the helmet signed by Len Dawson and Joe Montana that we received as a gift from fans in Tennessee. We also have several banners, footballs and other memorabilia that other fans have sent us. There's too much of an attachment to the Chiefs for us not to be fans.

**- LT. COL. BRIAN BIRDWELL**
**A Kansas City Chiefs fan who survived the attack**
**on The Pentagon, Sept. 11, 2001.**

# From '...the Land of the Free' To 'Oh, Baby, What a Play!'

*During their hey-day, the Chiefs were a regular part of the Monday Night Football schedule. But when you ask Chiefs fans about their most memorable MNF moment at Arrowhead Stadium, they all talk about Oct. 7, 1991, when former Chiefs coach Marv Levy brought his defending AFC champion Buffalo Bills to town and they were manhandled 33-6 by the Chiefs. Those fans sitting in the upper deck at Arrowhead Stadium talk about how the stands were actually moving from the pounding feet and hearts of 76,120 die-hard fanatics.*

## PATTI DIPARDO-LIVERGOOD
### Daughter of legendary Chiefs band leader Tony DiPardo and music director of the Tony DiPardo Pack Band.

Tony DiPardo and daughter Patti.
Photo courtesy of Scott E. Thomas Photography

From the moment we pulled into the Arrowhead Stadium parking lot for the first Monday Night Football Game at Arrowhead Stadium in eight years, I knew it was going to be different — be emotional, special, amazing — any adjective you want to use. Weeks before the game, (former Chiefs executive vice president) Tim Connolly had called me and asked if I would sing the National Anthem. Are you kidding? Of course! I had sung the anthem many times, but I knew that this night would be special – and it was. Tim had seen these amazing leather coats – all the players were wearing them back in 1991 – and he had one ordered just for me. It was red, white and blue, so darling. And it was perfect for that night. I still have it, although I was a size 4 back then. When we got out of the car, the electricity was felt in the parking lot. It was crackling. It was a perfect night for football. ▪

## DAN LESTER
### Former Independence police officer

I don't remember the date, but I remember the year – 1991. We hadn't been on a Monday Night Football game forever, and the Bills came to town and we kicked their butt. I remember how the stadium shook – I mean, it literally shook – with all the fans going so nuts. I remember Derrick Thomas having a big game, and how we had (Buffalo) quarterback Jim Kelley on his back the entire game. But the one thing that stands out for me was the National Anthem. Everyone sang it – and when it was done, the place went nuts. I think I remember that more than any part of the game." ▪

## TONY DIPARDO
### The Chiefs 97-year-old bandleader, who has been with the team from Game 1 at old Municipal Stadium.

It's impossible for me to talk about my favorite game because there have been so many of them. But one of my favorite moments came when my (daughter) Patti sang the National Anthem before that Chiefs Monday Night

Football game against the Buffalo Bills. She looked like Lady Liberty with her red, white and blue outfit and had on her white cowboy hat. She was just perfect – and so was the anthem. When she started singing, and 76,000 people inside Arrowhead joined the chorus, it was just one of those things you never forget. Then, the stadium just erupted in applause. I was so proud, the proudest dad at Arrowhead Stadium. ▪

## KEVIN HARLAN
### Kansas City Chiefs broadcaster from 1985 to 1993

People ask me how I came up with, "Oh, baby, what a play!" and to be honest with you, it just happened. The first time it was brought to my attention was after that Monday Night Football game against the Bills back in 1991. I was driving home with my wife, Annie, after the game and some fans called into the post game show. They were still in the parking lot, celebrating, and you could tell they'd had one or two too many. They were talking about the game, and they started counting down, "One, two, three – Oh, baby, what a play!" You know, it was probably 15 drunk guys having a good time out in the parking lot at Arrowhead Stadium, but they liked that line. I thought to myself, "I better use that line again." ▪

## BILL MAAS
### Chiefs Pro-Bowl nose tackle, who had two sacks in the game

That was the most electrifying game I was ever a part of at Arrowhead Stadium. We fed off the fans' energy the entire game. When I got out of my car in the parking lot before the game started and heard the buzz inside I knew it was going to be special. That's what it must have been like to have played for the Chiefs back in their glory years." ■

# Memories ...

I like everything about the new management team and coaching staff. The last two years (2007 and 2008) were pretty bad. I don't see how a team can finish with a 2-14 record after being near the top of the division for so many years, but it happened to the Chiefs last year. I think Herm Edwards wanted to be the players' friend instead of the coach, and that hurt him. I know there were many injuries. Believe me, coaching gymnastics, I know about injuries. And that was a big part of the team's problems last year. But I like the new approach this new staff has. You can tell they don't want to be anyone's friend; they want to build a football program and they want to win. And I know they will get this team back to its winning ways. Scott Pioli was part of that great New England team and I like Todd Haley, although he has upset some fans and players. That's fine with me. We need a coach who wants to coach, and not be friends with everyone. Look at Tony (Gonzalez, the team's all-pro tight end and the most productive player at that position in the history of the NFL), he didn't really seem like he wanted to play here and they traded him. They want players who want to be Kansas City Chiefs. That's the only way a coach can be a success is when he has players who want to be a part of the team. I am not at Arrowhead Stadium, but it seems the approach has changed and there is a new attitude and I think we're going to see a lot more wins this season because of it.

- AL FONG

**Coach of 2004 Olympic gymnastic silver medal winners Terin Humphrey and Courtney McCool from Great American Gymnastic Express in Blue Springs, Missouri, and the former United States Gymnastics Association Coach of the Year**

\* \* \*

I was at the game where my dad got seven sacks (against Seattle, to set an NFL single-game record in a 17-16 Seahawks victory over the Chiefs on a last-second TD pass from future Chiefs quarterback Dave Krieg). He came down and got me after the game and we went in the locker room and it was real quiet. He didn't even keep the seventh sack ball. He gave it to a friend of his because he never kept anything from a loss – not even the ball that set an NFL record. On the ride home, we didn't talk about the game at all. We just talked about other stuff like how I was doing in school – things like that."

- DERRION THOMAS

**An all-state senior linebacker from Blue Springs South High School and the son of late Chiefs Hall of Fame linebacker Derrick Thomas. Derrion had a five-sack game his senior year at South and led the Jaguars to the Class 6 state championship game.**

\* \* \*

The longest – and the most fun – 16 weeks of the year are the 16 weeks the Chiefs play. We have some regulars who usually beat us to the joint. They get here around 9 a.m. or so and we try to have their pizzas ready to go. It's

the crowd (former Cy Young Award winner) Rick
Sutcliffe hangs out with. We call them the Sugar Creek
crowd, and they leave their beer bottles all over the place
– so we have to go out and get rid of them before the
church crowd shows up around 11 when we open. We
have people who come in, we expect them – so their pizza
is ready and waiting – and they just sit in here and
watch the game and cheer like they're at Arrowhead.

**- STEVE PACE**

**Co-owner of Tim's Pizza, an iconic Independence eatery
that is a favorite of many Kansas City pro athletes,
executives and the common folks – like Rick Sutcliffe's
"Sugar Creek Crowd."**

* * *

Derrick (Thomas) loved our pizza. He lived just about a
half mile from our place and he'd stop and pick it up or
send over one of his friends – and that guy knew more
people than anyone I think I know. Big Daddy Carl
Hairston (a former Chiefs assistant coach) would come in
and pick up a big pizza after the home games and Dan
Saleamua would get a pizza after the games. I swear –
those two guys were bigger than the (vending) machines
we have. We love it when the fans come in and watch the
games, but I think our favorite time is early Sunday
morning when Rick (Sutcliffe) and his crew come in and
we make them a Sugar Creek cooler. That's a cardboard
box, lined with a plastic trash bag and filled with ice and
beer. I think they like the name as much as they do the
beer. We'd do anything for those guys and they'd do anything for us and they love the Chiefs and our pizza. It
was funny, someone once told Steve and me that they'd
rather watch the game here and eat our pizza than stand

in line with "78,000 of their best friends waiting to use the toilet at the stadium."

**- TIM PACE**
**Co-owner and founder of Tim's Pizza, the legendary**
**pizza joint that has been the hub of Independence**
**pizza and sports talk for the past 21 years.**

\* \* \*

When my buddy from college and I bought our season tickets back in 1967, I don't think either one of us thought we'd still be going to games today. But it's something we still look forward to – even though the game-day experience has really changed since the days at Municipal Stadium on 22nd and Brooklyn in downtown Kansas City. We had seats in the Wolf Pack – some portable bleachers they brought into left field (at the stadium that also housed Major League Baseball's Kansas City Athletics) and we sat on about the 10-yard line. I'm an old timer, but I call the Chiefs back then, the real Chiefs – Lenny (Dawson), Bobby Bell, Otis Taylor, Jim Lynch, Mike Garrett – goodness, I loved watching those guys play. We had the three best linebackers in the history of the game with Bell, (Willie) Lanier and (Jim) Lynch. And we had the best coach in Hank Stram. I remember a game where the running backs were hurt and he put (all-pro punter) Jerrell Wilson in at running back. I was there when (Washington defensive back) Pat Fischer had Otis' arm pinned to his side and he still caught a touchdown pass and I took the bus from a family Christmas gathering to the stadium to watch the longest game in AFL history – the Christmas Day game we lost to Miami. That game still hurts. I still feel for (kicker) Jan Stenerud because he missed a couple of field goals and still has that whammy. My favorite game each year is the Alumni Game when the old timers come back. Some of them can barely walk, but they come out on the field and I just wonder how many of today's fans even know who they are. I sit in a section where everyone is 20+ and 30+ season ticket holders and we know who they are. And we will always love them.

**- Dr. RICH PRINE**
**Longtime Blue Springs, Missouri, dentist who now teaches at the University of Missouri-Kansas City Dental School, and a 42-year season ticket holder.**

\* \* \*

**I** remember sitting in the stands back in the late 70s and early 80s when there were about 7,000 people. I tell that to people now and they don't believe it. I think most fans today think that Arrowhead always was full, and it wasn't. After we won the Super Bowl and lost the Christmas Day game back in 1971, things went downhill fast. You knew that Coach Stram loved his players and they all got old. I remember watching Lenny's (Dawson) final game. I loved Lenny. Everyone loved Lenny the Cool. The line was so protective, like Grunny (center Tim Grunhard) was of all the quarterbacks we had in the 90s. When we went to games it was a family affair. Our family had 12 season tickets and we used every one of them. After the horrible start to the 80s, the Chiefs got Marty (Schottenheimer) as their coach and things turned around. I remember a game from the 13-3 season when we were in the parking lot and a big U-Haul parked right next to us. When they parked, a bunch of high school age kids got out and they brought out a couch and set up a space in the parking lot like a living room. They told us they didn't have tickets, they just wanted to come out and experience the tailgating and the game-day experience. I never forgot that. I thought to myself, this place must be pretty special when kids want to come and sit in the parking lot just to experience what we get to experience every Sunday during the season.

**- TERESA CLUM**
Independence, Missouri, season-ticket holder and a member of Homeland Security.

\* \* \*

My wife, Cindy, and I had season tickets from 1991 until 1994. This was a great time to be a Chiefs fan. It's hard to pick out any one event that sticks in my mind so I think it might make more sense to tell you what I remember. I remember when tailgating became cool and we would show up three hours before a game and cook food for our friends from the ad department at *The Kansas City Star.* Everyone would pitch in and bring or cook something great.

I remember thinking Carl Peterson was a great showman with the jets flying over before games and KC Wolf trouncing on a "Raider Fan" at midfield before a game. I remember the amazing energy when the Chiefs were on defense and Derrick Thomas and Neil Smith were coming at the quarterback from both ends. We honestly believed a sack was possible on every play. I remember the guy with the full Indian head dress at the end of our row in section 305 who would not let us sit down or leave the game

**❝I remember when the tomahawk chop was cool and no one worried whether it might be offensive. ❞**
*– STEVE CURD, Publisher,* The Examiner, *in Eastern Jackson County.*

early. He was our cheerleader and made the games so much fun. I remember when the tomahawk chop was cool and no one worried whether it might be offensive. I never could figure out why it would be perceived as a knock on culture. I saw it as a compliment and still do.

I remember that winning was expected and anything less than a playoff appearance was a disappointing season. The culture, in my opinion, came from Marty Schottenheimer and we have never had it since he left.

**- STEVE CURD**
Publisher, *The Examiner*, in Eastern Jackson County.

\* \* \*

Lachelle Jackson
Photo courtesy of Scott E. Thomas Photography

Oh my God, I don't even know how to explain what a game-day experience is for me. I hate driving in a big crowd, so I take the bus to Arrowhead Stadium. And it's a lot of fun. I purchase a season bus pass and make sure that I'm always on the first bus that goes to the stadium. That's important to me – I have to be on that first bus. And I always am. Once we get on that bus, and the bus driver plays the Chiefs music – you know, the Chiefs and chopper music – and we all get into it. It's so much fun, it gets you in the mood for the game before you even get to the stadium. Then, you pull into the stadium and see all the cars and smell that barbeque and you know you're in for the time of your life. We get off the bus, and once the fans see I'm a Red Coater, they tell me to come over to their car or van and tailgate with them. It's like we're one big, happy family. If you think that's fun, just wait. The real fun begins when we go down the tunnel to the field to form the two lines the players run between when they are introduced. It's so loud down on the field you can't hear anything. It's like being under water when you're swimming. All you can hear is yourself breathing. It's something you have to experience to believe. Your heart is just pounding and the players run by and the game's about to begin and you just thank the good Lord that you're a Chiefs fan and you can experience something like this.

- LACHELLE JACKSON
Kansas City Chiefs Red Coater.

* * *

Margie Carder
Photo courtesy of Scott E.
Thomas Photography

Anyone who says they would rather watch a game on television than go to Arrowhead Stadium has either never been to Arrowhead or they are lying. The game-day experience is so unique, so special. We go to the games with the people we have always gone with. We get up at the crack of dawn and are among the first people there at 9 a.m. for a noon game. We tailgate out in the parking lot and the time just flies by. Before you know it, we're in the stadium, heading down onto the field. We form the tunnel for the players to run through going out onto the field before the game starts and it's electric. I mean it, it really is electric. You can't even talk to the person standing next to you it's so loud down there. All of the Red Coaters pick out a different player to watch when they run out (of the locker room/tunnel area) because some are more prone to give you a high-five or look your way. It's the perfect way to start a game. We make it an entire day, starting around 9 a.m. and going home around 5:30 p.m. It's the best time of the year for all of us.

**- MARGIE CARDER**
**Kansas City Chiefs Red Coater.**

\* \* \*

I went to my first Chiefs game in 1979 against the Denver Broncos and it was about 13 degrees below zero and I was hooked. I loved the atmosphere. I loved everything about the game. Since that game, I've only missed two home games and look forward to everything about the game-day experience. As a Red Coater, we do many wonderful things, including a lot of charity work that has become my favorite part of being a Red Coater. But for me, nothing tops forming the funnel the players run through as they go out onto the field before the start of the game. I usually try to stand in a different place every game just to see everything that happens on the field and in the stands. Over the years, we have had players like Eddie Kennison and Tony Gonzalez, who run through the funnel and slap hands or high-five the Red Coaters and that makes it very special. The electricity that runs through the stadium when the players come out and the game begins is hard to describe. You can't hear a thing and it's like an electric jolt goes through your body. I wish everyone could experience something like that. Once you do, you're a Chiefs fan for life.

**- MIKE EBENROTH**
**President of the Kansas City Chiefs Red Coaters.**

I was a pro football nut! I was in 1963 when the Chiefs first came to town and I am today, even though I'm 88 years old. I love the game and I love the Chiefs. When I heard back in 1963 that we were getting an American Football League team I didn't care who they were – I wanted tickets! I worked for Panhandle Eastern Pipe Line, and I knew the company was going to buy season tickets to give out to the employees, but I wanted my own ticket so I could go to every game. I rushed right out and bought my season ticket – and I think, now I'm not too sure, but I think they were $10 a game. I sat in section 118, row 25, seats 26 and 27. Over the next 36 years I missed three games – one because I was sick and the other two were work related and I was out of town. And you could park for about a dollar in the Sam's Parking lots. I never missed a game at the old stadium, not one. I even went to those silly Grocery Bowl games (featuring Chiefs rookies). It was football, and I didn't care who was playing. When I think back to the old days, I remember watching a young quarterback at Purdue named Len Dawson. We had an office in Crawfordsville, Indiana, which is about 27 miles south of Lafayette. I saw Len play five or six times when he was in college, so you know I was excited when I found out he was coming to town from Dallas. He was my hero before he even played in the NFL. Everyone in Kansas City loved Len Dawson. But I don't know if anyone loved that team as much as I did. I think I hated those Raiders as much as I loved the Chiefs. When that eight-ball Ben Davidson hit Lenny (in a famous spearing incident that resulted in a brawl on the field) I was so mad I wanted to fight someone myself. I didn't like that coach from Green Bay (Vince Lombardi) who said the AFL was a Mickey Mouse league. That made me mad. We didn't do very well against Green Bay in that first Super Bowl, but we came back and beat Minnesota in the fourth Super Bowl and I still remember the celebration we had in downtown Kansas City. I'd like to see another one of those celebrations, I really would.

**- CHARLES AMICK**
**Original Kansas City Chiefs season ticket holder.**

\* \* \*

**I** have the check I wrote to the Kansas City Chamber of Commerce for $98 encased in hard plastic. I think I did that because I knew it was going to be very special to me someday, and it really is very special. The date on the check is April 22, 1963, and it's made out to the Chamber of Commerce for football tickets. On the back, it's stamped "received by the Columbia National Bank." I remember so many things about the old stadium on Brooklyn and 22nd streets. There wasn't much parking, so we would go to games and park in someone's yard for fifty cents. And if you paid them an extra quarter or fifty cents, they promised that they would watch your car the entire game. It was mostly kids, and I don't know if they watched the cars or not, but they sure liked getting that extra fifty cents. My first seat was in the main part of the stadium, and we were pretty much protected from the elements. It used to snow back then at games, and it was nice to have the cover for protection. Then, they brought in those bleachers in left field of the baseball stadium and called it the Wolf Pack. My wife and I got seats out there and we were right next to War Paint – the horse that ran around the stadium after the Chiefs scored. I loved to watch that horse, and his rider had a war bonnet. I think they kept him out at Benjamin Stables.

He was probably the most famous horse in the AFL. There were some great games but the one I bet everyone talks about is the Christmas Day game in 1971. It was the longest game ever played and we had a lot of chances to win that game, but Miami came out on top with a field goal in the second overtime. I still love the Chiefs, but back then, we lived and died with them. It took a long time to get over that loss. That was the last game played in Municipal Stadium. The next year the team moved to Arrowhead and it was something to see. We all wondered where our seats would be in the new stadium and we were happy to see that they were three rows from the field right behind the Chiefs bench. I'm 85 now, and I kept my tickets through the 1998 season. I still watch the Chiefs on television and listen on the radio. I'm still a fan and always will be.

**- ALTON WILLIFORD**
**Original Kansas City Chiefs season ticket holder.**

\* \* \*

Even though I lived in Chicago for a few years during the 1990s, I made it to only one Bears game. That one game, however, was very memorable.

Unless you've been to a game at Soldier Field, you can't really tell but the stadium is right next to Burnham Harbor, where a lot of people who boat on Lake Michigan keep their crafts docked. During the exhibition season and in September before it turns cold, many of these folks will have tailgate parties on their boats. Some of them won't even go to the game, choosing rather to glide around on the water and watch the Bears on little portable televisions.

This particular season, the Chiefs were in town for a night exhibition game. My boss at the time had a boat in Burnham Harbor and decided to have a big football party on board. Some of us got tickets for the game, while others went just for the party. It was a beautiful, but unusually muggy day. A lot of people were swimming and otherwise enjoying the water. I was dispatched around lunch time to take a bunch of booze to the boat and set up a bar, as I had formal bartending experience. (I actually did this on company time and got paid for it!)

Gradually, people started to filter in and it was a nice little party and the bar did a robust business. Ours was only one of several little parties going on around the dock.

As game time approached, clouds had begun to move in and it was getting a little dark. The wind kicked up and was blowing like crazy. As a caravan of us made the sojourn over to Soldier Field, it began to sprinkle. We made it to our seats. My girlfriend, a big Chiefs' fan, was decked out in a Joe Montana Chiefs jersey and, of course, took a lot of verbal abuse. As the game moved on, the rain kept getting heavier and heavier. Thunder rolled in and just after halftime, it was a full-blown monsoon. Lightning was cracking everywhere and the rain was swirling in the strong wind so that you couldn't escape it. Of course, we were all so well-lubricated that we didn't mind. By the middle of the third quarter, you could barely see the field. The lightning was getting so bad that they called the game. A football game, mind you. I remember being incredulous that they would call a football game.

With all of us soaked to the bone, we leaned into the storm and made our way back to the boat. Most of the revelers had headed home but there were a few stalwarts who stuck it out. We joined them and re-opened the bar. The storm kept getting worse and before I knew it, I realized that despite the lightning flashing all around the water and the docks, there were people swimming. Not just off our boat, but other boats as well. I remember commenting about how precarious it was to be in the water at that time but, of course, I ended up jumping in as well. Thankfully, no one was fried. No, the game itself wasn't overly memorable, but what a night!

**- BRAD DOOLITTLE**

\* \* \*

Over the years, I've had many memorable experiences with the Chiefs. Our relationship goes back to the make-up game against the New York Jets in December 1963, the team's first year in Kansas City, after President Kennedy was assassinated. I was in college at the time, on Christmas break, and my dad took me. We both froze our feet in the ice-encrusted Wolf Pack section during our 48-0 win.

Then there were the thrills of personally witnessing our underdog Super Bowl victory at Tulane Stadium in New Orleans as well as earning my Red Coat the following year.

But my greatest Chiefs' memories came from the time that my wife, Jan, and I were privileged to accompany the Chiefs and their entourage on their charter trip to the World Bowl Game in Tokyo, Japan, in August 1994. The trip started out at a high level when, during the flight, Derrick Thomas came up to our section of the 747 and helped the cheerleaders sew sequins on their costumes, followed by the reception we got at the hotel by all of the Japanese children wanting autographs from quarterback Joe Montana. But the best from that trip was yet to come.

One evening during the days leading up to the game, we took a harbor dinner cruise with the team. While we were waiting to board our ship, a very large contingent of Japanese gathered in the same waiting area where our group was. This obviously was a serious family reunion. They had a photographer with them, who diligently lined them up in tiered rows for a major formal family photo. After much effort, they finally were ready for the picture to be taken. At the very last mini-second, Marcus Allen hopped on the end of the last row just as the flash went off. Can you imagine the reaction when the picture was developed and this huge, totally unfamiliar darker-skinned gentleman appeared in it? We have a picture of the posed group with Marcus in it and still get a laugh out of it.

The other great memory of that evening was the scene of a Dixieland Jazz Band made up of elderly Japanese men parading around the ship led by Derrick Thomas and Neil Smith belting out "When the Chiefs Come Marching In."

On a somber note, I'll never forget, as a Red Coater volunteer, assisting with the open coffin memorial for Derrick Thomas at Arrowhead Stadium on Valentine's Day, 2000. The outpouring of people and their emotions that day was one of the most profound and powerful sensations I've ever felt.

I've had a lot of fabulous memories of the Chiefs, but those were clearly the most vivid of them all.

**- ALLAN BLOCK**

\* \* \*

Every Chiefs game has become a holiday in the Wissel/Maloney family – EVERY game! It also happened to be a family member who helped me have my biggest memory as a Chiefs' fan. The first game I ever attended was in November 1976, shortly after I turned 7 years old. My uncle took one of my younger brothers, Scott, and me to the Chiefs-Steelers game. At the time, the Chiefs weren't very good. The Steelers were awesome.

The kicker for me, and my younger brother, was that in an effort to save a buck, my uncle parked somewhere near the Fellowship of Christians Athletes building. (In case you're not familiar with the stadium, the FCA building is the one across Interstate 70 that you can see beyond left field at Kauffman Stadium.) I remember walking down this huge hill, over the interstate and then what seemed like two more miles over to Arrowhead. The walk back wasn't any fun, either.

The Chiefs were absolutely annihilated 45-0 by the likes of Terry Bradshaw, Franco Harris, Lynn Swann, Jack Lambert, Mean Joe Green, etc. (Man, were all those guys really on the same team?!)

The only Chiefs player that stood out for me that day was our third-string quarterback, Mike Nott, just because I liked the number 7. That was his only season with the Chiefs. That day may have been the only NFL game he played.

As with most Chiefs fans, I have many other great memories from games. For instance, in 2003 when Dante Hall broke off his 97-yard punt return against the Broncos. That was the loudest that I have ever heard Arrowhead Stadium.

Another great Chiefs memory was during my college days in Quincy, Illinois. One of my best college buddies, Mark Trapp, was a huge Broncos fan. The two of us watched every Chiefs-Broncos game together like it was the Super Bowl. Those Chiefs wins were very sweet for me and the losses were the worst! My hatred for the Broncos was at an all-time high when Trapp was around.

In fact, the coldest I have ever been in my entire life might have been at Arrowhead when the Chiefs played the Patriots. I was so excited that someone gave me Chiefs tickets. Little did I know what was to come. The week of the game brought snow, and the day of the game brought freezing rain. Snow was sitting in the aisles, so we had our feet on top of snow, and then we were drenched by the freezing rain, with dropping temperatures. That was the only Chiefs game that I bailed on at halftime. I seriously thought I was going to lose my toes to frost bite.

In the summer of 2004, I took a job in Cincinnati, moving away from Kansas City and the Chiefs for the only time besides college. I miss the weekly Wissel/Maloney festivities. But I won't ever miss walking across I-70 to park.

**- JIM WISSEL**

\* \* \*

I am a lifelong Chiefs fan. I was raised in Paola, Kansas, in a family of Chiefs fans. Before Arrowhead was built, my father gave my mother Chiefs season tickets as an anniversary gift and she was thrilled. To this day our extended family sets the date for our Christmas celebration based in part on my firefighter cousins' work schedules and in part on whether the Chiefs play on Saturday or Sunday any given December weekend.

I remember going to games as a child and taking a large garbage bag to stand in (they do keep your legs incredibly warm) and a carpet square to stand on. Somehow in my mind the last home game of the season and the coldest game of the year was always the Broncos game. To this day, I remember my mom having to explain signs to me that fans had brought. "Santa Claus, the Chiefs think Brian is Griese kid's stuff" is still my favorite for creativity and cramming multiple references into one sign.

But there's nothing like being a Chiefs' fan in another part of the country. In the fall of 1993, I was living in Grand Rapids, Michigan. This was the first time in my life that I had lived outside the Chiefs' broadcast area. The only way to get Chiefs' games was to invest in a satellite dish or go to a restaurant/bar called Damon's. I became a regular at Damon's on Sunday afternoons. They had four huge screens and one always showed the Chiefs. One September Sunday, my husband (a converted Chicago Bears' fan) and I were in Damon's. I was wearing my usual red and gold when I noticed another patron similarly clad.

Like true survivors of adversity, we became instant friends. Chiefs' fans, stranded in alien territory, had to stick together. As it turned out, my new friend was from Ottawa, Kansas, and had been in 4-H with one of my closest friends from college. The local Grand Rapids weatherman was a University of Missouri graduate and also a Chiefs fan. So, we gathered at Damon's every Sunday that fall to watch games together and continued to socialize after football season.

My oldest son was born in November 1995 in New Jersey. He was three days old when he first donned his Chiefs apparel for a Sunday game. My mom had come to help and brought red insulated underwear, Chiefs socks and a Chiefs hat for Jackson. We have at least a dozen pictures of him sleeping through his first game. He is destined to be a true fan; he slept through his second game five days later on Thanksgiving. "Go Chiefs" was one of Jackson's first phrases. He and his younger brother learned the "chop" at an early age.

We moved to Detroit in the spring of 1996. Imagine my delight at the prospect of watching the Chiefs play the Lions on Thanksgiving. I purchased tickets immediately. It hadn't occurred to me that we might have trouble finding a baby sitter on Thanksgiving. I had to consider the prospect of taking our 1-year-old son to the game. That Thanksgiving, I discovered what ear infections do to small children. Jackson spiked a fever well over 102 and acetaminophen wasn't touching it. I spent Thanksgiving with a sick and cranky toddler while my husband (that converted Bears fan, no less!) and his friend (a hockey fan!) watched the Chiefs bury the Lions.

The next fall, while still in Detroit, I watched the Chiefs play the Broncos on Monday Night Football. The game didn't start until quite late; we were in the Eastern Time zone. My husband (did I mention that he used to be a Bears fan?) was not interested in watching the game. He went to sleep! There I was with a wonderful game and no one with whom to discuss it. I checked the time and realized that though it was well past 9:00 in Detroit, it wasn't in KC. I called my dad to discuss a play. My father loves the Chiefs, but is their toughest critic. Later during the first quarter, he called me to discuss another play. By game's end, we had called back and forth at least seven times. We were both still awake, full of adrenaline and pleased with the end result. I was ecstatic. Dad, the football pessimist, felt they were lucky. For me, it was a big game. I had discovered that I could still share football with my family no matter how far apart we were.

I'm back in the Kansas City area now, but my parents and I rarely watch football together anymore. However, when the phone rings during Chiefs' games, they answer with, "Yes, Shari, we saw that." And I know that no one is likely to call me during a game except them.

**- SHARI HENRICKSON**

* * *

Back in 1971, we were like the rest of the city, busy planning a Christmas holiday around the Chiefs playoff game against Miami. Two days before the game, I was a bored 9-year-old, sitting in the back of the family station wagon with my 13-year-old brother at Kansas National Bank in Prairie Village, while my Dad ran into the bank to get some Christmas shopping money.

Dad returned from the bank, all excited because he had seen coach Hank Stram inside (probably getting money for another snappy sports coat to wear on the sidelines). Dad, a lifelong Cleveland Browns fan, and a recent 100 percent convert to Chiefs fandom, decided that he couldn't pass up the opportunity to wish Coach Stram luck in the upcoming game. Unfortunately for my brother and me, it was about 20 degrees outside and we were waiting in the back of a freezing station wagon because the heater wouldn't reach the very back of the car. The middle seat was reserved for a sister that was already passed out from an exhausting day of shopping.

Apparently, Coach Stram had business to do inside because he didn't come out for about 15 minutes. My Mom was begging Dad to hurry up before my brother and I froze to death. Anyway, like a hungry shark circling his prey, Dad refused to leave, but he agreed to drive around the parking lot until Hank came out. Finally, Dad's moment arrived when Hank came out to his car. Dad pulled up alongside Hank's car, leaned out the window, and very loudly wished him luck in the game against Miami. He punctuated his wishes with the phrase "GIVE 'EM HELL, HANK!" Hank, being the classy guy that he was, waved at Dad and told him, "Thanks!" Dad was pretty pleased with himself and knew that his well-wishes would put his beloved Chiefs over the top.

Well, we know what happened. The Chiefs lost 27-24. However, being a family with a wicked sense of humor, my brother and mother jokingly suggested that the use of the word "hell" that close to Christmas probably had lost the game for the Chiefs. I think for about five days, my distraught father actually believed it. But the best part is that using the phrase "Give 'Em Hell, Hank!" became a family joke (at Dad's good-natured expense, of course) and would be pulled out whenever some kind of disaster would befall the family. Example: The day the dishwasher broke and gushed water all over the kitchen floor in 1974 was greeted with a hearty "Give 'Em Hell, Maytag!" by my brother when we walked into the house and saw "Lake Rose."

It's safe to say that 99 percent of my Chiefs memories are happy ones. Even Dave Krieg escaping Derrick Thomas' grasp (for what would have been his eighth sack of the day) and firing a game-winning touchdown pass was STILL a damn exciting game and a great (if painful) memory.

But my most vivid memory of the Chiefs took place in the fall of 2000. My father had been battling cancer for almost two years (we lost my Mom in February of 1999 to cancer), and he was spending his last days at home with a hospice nurse taking care of him. He was slipping further and further down, but he was basically pain-free and comfortable. Before the cancer, he was a vivacious, burly 6'2" sales executive that had a joke for any occasion and a permanent smile on his face – especially when it came to his Chiefs. He definitely was very alert and knew everything that was going on when he was awake. In week four of that season, the Chiefs traveled to Denver to take on the Broncos. Any Chiefs fan can tell you that the Chiefs' luck in Denver was bad, bad, bad ... and there wasn't any reason to believe it was going to change that season.

I went over to Dad's house to watch the game with him on TV, but he was too tired to get out of bed, so we listened to Mitch Holthus, Lenny Dawson, Bob Gretz and the bee-uuu-tee-ful Bill Grigsby on the radio. For three hours, I laid on Dad's bed, holding his hand as we chatted about 33 years of Chiefs memories: how

> **❝I kissed him on the forehead and told him good-bye, and as he turned over, he gave me a thumbs-up and said, "Go Chiefs!" A few hours later, I received a call from the hospice nurse who told me that Dad had slipped into a coma. ❞**
> – DAN WILSON
> *A lifetime Chiefs fan and season ticket holder who first went to games sitting on his father's lap.*

much he missed going to Arrowhead; how much he missed Mom and her Gameday Chili; and how much Lenny Dawson reminded him of Otto Graham. The Chiefs and Gunther Cunningham beat the Broncos that day and when Mitch excitedly counted down the end of the game, Dad tried to put up his hand for our traditional "Game-Winning High Five" that we had done so many times since I was 4 years old.

I told him that I'd be back the next week to listen to the game with him, which prompted a stern, very Dad-like, "The Seahawks are in town for Monday Night Football and you will NOT miss it!" I told him that I had already given the tickets to my teenage son and his friends, so they wouldn't go to waste. He smiled and told me that his grandson using the tickets was acceptable. We laughed about it and then he told me that he was really tired out from the game and that I needed to get home to my family. I kissed him on the forehead and told him good-bye, and as he turned over, he gave me a thumbs-up and said, "Go Chiefs!"

A few hours later, I received a call from the hospice nurse who told me that Dad had slipped into a coma. Four days later, he passed away, but I can't help but smile when I think of a better way for he and I to have spent our last time together ... listening to Mitch, Lenny, Bob and Bill describing a Chiefs victory over the Broncos.

Go Chiefs!

**- DAN WILSON**
A lifetime Chiefs fan and season ticket holder who first went to games sitting on his father's lap.

I guess since I was a rodeo cowboy, I fit the bill of what the Chiefs were looking for back in 1963. They wanted a cowboy on a horse, so I put on a war bonnet and got on

Warpaint and off we went. I was at every home game –
and the two Super Bowls – between 1963 and 1989. It
was a great run and I had a lot of fun with it. The game
was so different back then. I had acreage out in eastern
Jackson County and I put in a little golf course and then
a softball field. All the guys would come over and play.
Al Reynolds and Ed Buddle loved playing softball. We
had a good time on the field and off the field. I was just
an ol' cowboy and we all got along together. I think early
on, more people came to see Warpaint than they did the
Chiefs. But that changed quickly. The fans in Kansas
City didn't know what to expect early on and neither did
I. But boy, did they become a great team. They had a
great owner in Mr. Hunt, and talk about great players!
They had an all-star at just about every position on the
field. I'd ride Warpaint hell-bent for leather every time
the Chiefs scored. I remember when we beat Chicago (66-
24 in 1967) in an exhibition game and Dick Butkus said,
"We damn near killed that horse." And he was right. I
am proud to say that I have seen every game at home, on
the road, or on television since the team came to town. I
loved being a part of the team. I'll never forget the time
I rode by (bandleader) Tony DiPardo and said, "Come on,
Tony, we're going for a ride." It was the first – and
probably the last – time he ever got on a horse. Tony was
holding on for dear life. Everyone loved it!

**- BOB JOHNSON**
**The rodeo cowboy who rode Warpaint, the Chiefs mascot,**
**from 1963 to 1989.**

\* \* \*

I've never been a big autograph hound, but I enjoy
watching the looks on the fans' faces as they come to our
place to meet the players. I'm proud to say that we did

the last autograph signing with Derrick Thomas, and he's going into the Pro Football Hall of Fame this year (2009). It was December 21, 1999, and Derrick was one of those players who made each fan feel special. I wish I could say that about all the guys, but he was just more personable than a lot of the players who would come sign. I think Derrick

> What do you say to a Raiders fan with a job?
>
> "I'll have fries with that."

enjoyed it as much as the fans, especially the kids. He'd joke around with them and take photos and everyone had a great time. A guy who got a bad rap in Kansas City was Andre Rison, but when he did a signing he was just like Derrick. I remember one little guy who came in a wheelchair and he went over and posed for a photo and took him out of the wheelchair – it was really touching. When you have a place like this, you see the real fans and I think that players like Derrick and Andre would come here because they liked being with the fans.

**- PETE CATALANO**

**Co-owner of Sports Nutz, a memorabilia and sporting goods store.**

\* \* \*

A group of us young guys went to the first Super Bowl game in Los Angeles and we took this big hammer we made, because Fred "The Hammer" Williamson had all but guaranteed a Chiefs victory. He was a colorful guy so we wanted to support him. We had a layover in Las Vegas and we spray-painted that hammer red right in our hotel room. Somewhere in Vegas, there is probably a red outline of a big hammer on the floor of a hotel room. We left for the game, and our plane was late and by the time we would have gotten there, Williamson had been knocked unconscious, so all our hard work was for nothing. I think we just left the thing in the cab. That was just a great memory, even though the Chiefs lost the game. But one of my greatest memories came when Mr. Hunt dropped by our store before a game. He just came up and said hello and had some mustard on his shirt. He'd just gotten a hamburger or something and got a little mustard on his shirt, so we got him another shirt. He was just such a gracious and wonderful man. We gave him a carousel made out of Chiefs mini-helmets and he was just speechless. Watching him look at that carousel just made me smile. It was great to give something back to a man who has given so much to our community.

**- PHIL MORREALE**
**Co-owner of Sports Nutz, a memorabilia and sporting goods store.**

**\* \* \***

I don't think this story has ever been in print. At least, I know I've never told it to anyone – and it's a good one. When we had the Italian Gardens downtown, my cousin, Vince, and I were working late one night. It was about 10 or so and we were about to close when 17 people walk in – there were 16 men and one very attractive woman. We put some tables together so they could all sit together as a group and I kept wondering, who are these people? The men were very athletic looking and a good looking group of guys. I just had to know what they were doing in town. So I went up and started talking to them. The guy with the woman introduced the guys at the table as the Dallas Texans. I didn't even know who the Dallas Texans were – and what were they doing in our restaurant? I found out that night that I was talking to Len Dawson. He was there with his wife and he told me that the Texans were coming to Kansas City, although it wasn't official yet and hadn't been announced. "We're moving to Kansas City," Lenny said. And I thought, well, we're getting a football team. These guys sure look like they can play. I don't remember all the guys who were there that night, but Lenny was there and Johnny Robinson and Abner Haynes. You know, after a while Lenny started doing the sports for Channel 9 and their studios were right down the street from our restaurant. He'd come in every week or so and we'd sit down and talk about football and I'd remind him of that first time he came in with all his Dallas Texan teammates. Now, that was a night to remember."

**- CARL DiCAPO**
The former restaurateur lives on Carl DiCapo Drive in
downtown Kansas City.

\* \* \*

I was sitting in the Arrowhead Stadium parking lot, tailgating with my friends, when I see a golf cart with a couple of men coming toward my bus. I look a little bit closer and see that Lamar Hunt and Jack Steadman are in the golf cart. Mr. Hunt gets out and asks, "Where's Steve Gildehaus?" I was shocked. I didn't know what to think. I told him that I was Steve Gildehaus and he spent the next 45 minutes talking with me about the team, eating a hot dog or hamburger, and having a soda. The girls in the office arranged everything because my bus had been voted "Best of Show" for two years in a row. It was a contest the Chiefs had for fans who came to Arrowhead in a bus or van that was decorated with Chiefs colors. I went all out with my bus – it was painted in the Chiefs colors, it had 12 first-class seats, a big-screen TV, a bar, a grill – we had the United States flag, a Chiefs flag and, of course, a Grain Valley flag. Tailgaiting is so special for me and my friends. I've had up to 35 season tickets and have never had less than 20 people go to the games with me and my family. We have friends come in from out of town and we want to do it up right. Fred Arbanas and Curtis McClinton have stopped by to sign the bus and Jack Steadman and Mr. Hunt also signed it. We get to the stadium when the gates open and usually leave about 1-1/2 to 2 hours after the game is over. We just enjoy each other's company and sit around before the game and eat and drink and talk about the game, then, after it's over, we talk about the game itself. The Sundays the Chiefs are home are so special for me. I am more than a fan; I guess you could call me a fanatic. We've been going to all the games about 20 years – and we'll keep going another 20 years, God willing. They're the greatest show in town."

**- STEVE GILDEHAUS**
**Grain Valley developer, philanthropist, and Chiefs fan.**

\* \* \*

**I** wonder if anyone has ever spent their 50th birthday on the 50-yard line at Arrowhead Stadium? Well, thanks to some of my great former employees at Hallmark, I was able to do just that. My team at Hallmark surprised me on my 50th birthday with a gift I will always remember. I walked into my office and they handed me a card. Then, they blindfolded me and led me down to a sedan. We drove around and I had no idea where I was going. It was kind of like a scene from "Goodfellas," although I was hoping it would have a happy ending. Toward the end of the drive, we went down a long driveway – at the time I thought it was a driveway – and our long drive from downtown came to an end. When I stepped out of the sedan, I felt like I was standing on grass. And I was – the grass of Arrowhead Stadium. We had driven down the long tunnel from the players' parking lot, right onto the field and the 50-yeard line. Wow! What a way to celebrate the big 5-0! I had my picture taken at the 50 and then we went up to the press box for lunch. While I was eating, they had arranged for my boss and Hallmark CEO Donald Hall to call and ask, "Where on earth are you?" They said I was missing a critical meeting – but it was all part of their plan. Boy, they thought of everything. It was a birthday I will never forget.

### - JIM WELCH

**The author of *Grow Now*, Welch is a member of Five Star Speakers and the National Speakers Association. Before his retirement from Hallmark, he was the senior vice president of marketing.**

\* \* \*

**M**y mom wanted me to go shopping for some school clothes and I didn't want any part of it. I was about 12 and the last thing I wanted to do was spend the day shopping for clothes at Independence Center. The first store we went to was the Jones Store. My dad came along and we noticed this big crowd of people over in the men's department, near one of the cashiers. We knew something had to be happening, so we walked over there and saw Eric Warfield, a defensive back for the Chiefs. Now, you can imagine – I'm 12, I'm shopping, which I hate, and now I see one of my favorite Chiefs players – so I get pretty excited. I wanted to get his autograph, but I didn't have anything for him to sign. So I went out into the food court area and got a napkin. I got a pen from my mom and I went up to him and asked him for his autograph. I found out the reason all the people were gathered around him. There was something wrong with the cash register and he was waiting there to pay for some things he'd bought. I asked him to sign the napkin and he kind of looked at me and said, "Is that what you want me to sign?" I said it was all I had. Heck, I didn't know I was going to see a Chiefs player. So he went over and took a Chiefs hat off the wall and came back to me. He paid for it, signed it, and gave it to me – and I still have it today. I couldn't believe it. He bought the hat so he could sign it and give it to me. It meant a lot more than a signed napkin.

**- COREY FRANK**

**Truman High School senior and correspondent for "The Sonic Locker Room Show," a radio program that features players and coaches from his high school.**

**\* \* \***

It was Thanksgiving Day 2007 and I was more excited about going to see the Chiefs play the Broncos than I was a turkey dinner. I brought my friend Tyler, and I saw another friend named Levi. That was back when Larry Johnson was really good and we had a sign that read LJ=MVP. We were all down by the field, trying to get the players' attention. A security lady came over and said that sometimes, Eddie Kennison brings kids down on the field before the game. We were all excited because it was a nationally televised game and we thought that Eddie might take us down on

Where do Raider fans hold their get-togethers?

In Cellblock D.

the field. He came out on the field and was looking right at us and came over and took me and Levi down on the field. Was I dreaming? I'd never been on the field before, and I here I was on the field with Eddie Kennison on Thanksgiving. Eddie even gave me a football that had been used in a game. I kept thinking in my head that this has to be a dream. Tyler didn't get to go on the field, but Eddie came over and shook his hand. After that game, I went home and wrote him a letter and thanked him for taking me on the field and giving me the football. Sometimes I still think it's a dream – then I look over at my football he gave me and I know it's all real.

**- BLAKE ROBERTS**
**A 13-year Blue Springs resident who attends**
**Moreland Ridge Middle School.**

\* \* \*

Two of the most gracious hosts I've ever been around are Clark and Lamar Hunt. I've been a Red Coater for a long time and have missed just two games since Arrowhead Stadium opened. In 2005, Clark and Lamar invited about 40 Red Coaters to their homes when the Chiefs played the Cowboys in Dallas. We had hors d'oeuvres at Clark's home and then went to Lamar's home for dinner. Lamar's home was very nice, but modest. Each room had a theme – with furniture from Spain, Africa, England, Japan – and as far as football, I just saw a couple of little trophies that looked like they were from high school. Jerry Jones (the owner of the Dallas Cowboys) is one of Lamar's neighbors and they live on Preston Street. They have the Preston Street Trophy, which is a little bit like the Governor's Cup in Missouri, except it's just a little trophy that goes between Jerry and Lamar. Jerry had the trophy since the Cowboys won the last time the two teams played, but Jerry told Lamar he could borrow it if he wanted to. It was a night I will never forget.

**- KEN MARRS**
**Longtime member of the Red Coaters and a season ticket holder who lives in Liberty, Missouri.**

\* \* \*

**M**y mom used to work at a hotel and got to know a lot of the Chiefs players. We became good friends with Walter White and he would come over to our home to

Fred Gunn
Photo courtesy of Scott E. Thomas Photography

have Thanksgiving dinner with us. I was about 15, and you can imagine how thrilling that was for me. When I graduated from high school, I got passes to go onto the field before a game. I saw Walter and Henry Marshall and J.J. Smith. I saw my dad up in the stands and he gave me a camera. He told me to go get a photo of one of the members of the team the Chiefs were playing that Sunday

afternoon. The team was – THE RAIDERS! I thought my dad was nuts, but I got up the nerve to ask Otis Sistrunk if I could take his picture. Now, this was before the game, and he looked at me and said, "Get the f___ away from me." That was just about the response I expected. Next I asked "The Tooz," John Matuszak. He was crazier than Otis Sistrunk, but I asked him anyway and he looked at me and posed. He was going on the field and he just looked at me and let out a big roar-r-r-r-r! I took the picture and my dad was just going crazy up in the stands. I still have that picture. It's a little bit out of focus, but that's because my hands were shaking so badly. You can see Matuszak with that crazy look on his face. It was perfect.

**- FRED GUNN**

**Longtime season ticket holder, a volunteer with the Chiefs Ambassadors, and the operations manager at S&K Industries.**

\* \* \*

I went to a 10-year high school reunion and a buddy of mine I hadn't seen since we graduated came up to me and said, "I'm glad to see you're still alive. Your old man was so crazy watching those Chiefs games I was afraid he might have killed you if they lost." My dad was that passionate about the Chiefs. He was a yeller and a screamer. But it helped me prepare for pledging a fraternity because no one in that fraternity could scream louder than my dad. How ironic is it that now, I work for the Chiefs."

**- BRIAN JOHNSTON**

**Kansas City Chiefs sales manager.**

\* \* \*

The maddest I've ever been in my life was at a Chiefs game. It was 1968 and we were playing the Raiders. I love the Chiefs. I mean, I LOVE THE CHIEFS. But I hated the Raiders. I hated the Raiders as much as I loved the Chiefs. Ben Davidson speared Lenny Dawson and Otis Taylor tried to defend Lenny and took a swing at Big Ben. Well, the referee called a personal foul on the Chiefs and I went freaking ballistic. I was ranting and raving and screaming and yelling. I was so damned mad that I went home and wrote a letter to (then-NFL commissioner) Pete Rozelle and told him what a horse-bleep call that was. That official was relieved of his duties and I got a letter back from Pete and I still have it. God, I loved watching the team back at Municipal Stadium. We had seats in Stenerud's Roost. When they moved to Arrowhead, we got stuck up in the upper deck in the end zone. That was all right, I guess. They had to put us somewhere. I just know that being in Kansas City back when the Chiefs were the real Chiefs was pretty special. A buddy called me up and asked me if I wanted to go to Super Bowl IV. He said he could get some tickets for $180 and I said sure. Well, we get to New Orleans and they're playing the game at Tulane Stadium and there are guys outside the stadium selling tickets for $15. We didn't care; we just wanted to see the game. After the Chiefs won, we went to the team hotel and I told the security guy that we were friends of Jerrell Wilson, the Chiefs punter. I had been in the reserves with Jerrell, but he had no idea I was coming down for the game. The security guy said, "If you're friends with Jerrell, go on in." There we were, in the middle of the Chiefs Super Bowl victory party and we see Jerrell and he comes over and says, "What the hell are you doing here?" He had a big smile on his face and we partied away. I was 29 years old and having the time of my life."

**- DENNIS JOHNSTON**
**Father of Brian Johnston and a longtime fan and season**
**ticket holder.**

\* \* \*

I've avoided getting a real job for a long, long time. This will be my 20th season as KC Wolf and I'm proud to say that I have enjoyed every minute of every game at Arrowhead Stadium. I was Truman the Tiger at Missouri, and I was even Fred Bird at Busch Stadium (in St. Louis). But now, I just think of myself as KC Wolf. When I was contacted by the Chiefs, I didn't really know what to do. My family is from St. Charles, Missouri, and I had spent most of my life on the east side of the state. But I went to Arrowhead for an interview, and what's that they say? "The rest is history." I had one question when I was interviewed: Why is the Chiefs mascot a wolf? They told me about the history of the team and about the Wolf Pack at old Municipal Stadium so I began to create the KC Wolf personality. We'd drag a stuffed football player out onto the field in the beginning and I would do a belly flop on him and we got a big response. I thought, "We're onto something here." Then, we played the Raiders and I talked a friend of mine into wearing a Raiders jersey and going out onto the field waving a Raiders flag and I rode out on my Harley Davidson and I was wearing my leather jacket and they were playing "Bad to the Bone," on the PA system. I pounded him and the crowd went crazy. I was a little bit worried about fan reaction, especially since I make a lot of appearances at churches, but everyone loved it. Now, I make about 325 to 350 appearances a year – sometimes I might make as many as seven in a day. I've been to Tokyo twice, was at the 1990 Berlin game between the Chiefs and the Los Angeles Rams, and I have been to five or six Pro Bowl games in Hawaii. It can be pretty demanding – especially on those hot, early-season games, where I can lose 10 or 12 pounds. But I love it and I can't imagine doing anything else.

**- DAN MEERS**
**The Kansas City Chiefs mascot who has become an NFL icon.**

* * *

As a fan that was born and raised just 50 miles north of Denver, Colorado, I have spent 25 years being abused by Bronco fans. But NEVER for a moment have I considered being anything but a loud, proud Chiefs fan.

My earliest memory as a Chiefs' fan was when I was 5 years old and was in tap dance classes. My instructor requested that I do a solo performance at our recital. I was taught a routine by a former Solid Gold dancer who later became a choreographer for the Denver Bronco cheerleaders. My fanatical Chiefs parents decided that it would not be enough for me to wear just any old cheerleader uniform, so my mom had a Chiefs cheerleader uniform made for me. I had red and yellow pom-poms and even red and yellow puffs on my shoes. To this day, the video tape of that performance is one of my dad's favorites to show at parties. It is quite funny because on the tape you can hear other parents in the crowd wondering why this little blonde girl would be wearing a Chiefs' outfit instead of the Broncos. Twenty years later my dad found a porcelain doll with little blonde curls wearing a Chiefs' cheerleading uniform holding red and yellow pom-poms.

As a kid growing up my mom always thought that it was important that our neighbors knew which side of the fence we were on, so the first house that I can remember living in HAD to be painted red with yellow trim. When I turned 16, my mom gave me her Subaru that she had painted Arrowhead Red. Later that year we bought a Volkswagen Cabriolet and painted it KC yellow. We have since sold both, but the VW still is being driven around town with the KC arrowhead sticker melted onto the rear window.

Even though I was able to get Marcus Allen's autograph after a game one year in Denver, I'll never forget an experience around Christmas when I was about 17. That year, we went to Kansas to see my grandparents, which was nothing unusual. But this particular year, my parents were especially anxious to open gifts, even though Christmas was a few days away. There was one gift that my parents could not wait for me to open. I opened it and it was the cutest little bear dressed as a Chiefs football player. I thanked them and then put the bear aside to open the next gift. My parents were so excited about the bear that they made me open his box and take him out. I couldn't understand what the big deal was but I did it anyway. That is when I saw them tucked in his pants ?... the tickets to my first game at Arrowhead. It was the last home game of the season against the Seattle Seahawks. I was so excited I couldn't sleep. We left early the next morning and drove across the entire state to Kansas City. I had never seen anything like the stadium in my life. We stayed at the hotel next to the stadium and I could see it from my window. The morning after we arrived we went shopping and could not believe that EVERY store in the mall carried Chiefs' stuff. We had never gotten Chiefs stuff that didn't have to be ordered or picked up by friends going through Kansas City. (For some reason, Chiefs items aren't a hot commodity in Colorado.) That day, spending more money than one family should, we bought everything from blankets and jackets to gloves, boxer shorts, temporary tattoos and coffee mugs.

**- LACEE WILSON**

**A Greeley, Colorado, native and Kansas City Chiefs football fan who runs a Chiefs watch party in her native state – much to the chagrin of Bronco fans.**

* * *

One year, 101.1 the FOX radio station held a contest and named a Chiefs Fan of the Week every week at the Thursday night radio show. Chiefs' broadcaster Mitch Holthus gave that fan a nickname. My nickname is Snowstorm Sandy, and it was given to me as a result of this story.

On October 22, 1995, the Chiefs played the Broncos in Denver at Mile High Stadium. It was the game where Marcus Allen got his 100th touchdown. What was just as memorable for the fans that were there was the snowstorm that day. We had taken a Chiefs Travel Bus Trip to Denver for the game. We arrived on Saturday, and the weather was perfect, about 70 degrees and sunny. As Bill Grigsby would say: A beeuuutiful fall day. We were hanging out at the Chiefs hotel, having a great time seeing the players and meeting other Chiefs fans. Everyone kept talking about the snowstorm that was coming in from the west, and would be arriving sometime during the game. We had a hard time believing it could be anything significant. But as the evening wore on, the forecasts grew more ominous, and we started to take them more seriously. We ended up at the all-night K-Mart, buying boots, hand-warmers and ponchos (had to get the clear ones, because everything else said Broncos on it). We found ourselves in the checkout line with several other Chiefs fans making the same purchases.

By game time, it was overcast, and the temperature was dropping, but still nothing significant. Then, around halftime, it started to snow ... and snow ... and snow ... and snow ... big ... thick ... wet flakes. It was snowing so hard that they had people on the field at the 10-yard lines, who would run across after every play to clear the lines off with shovels so the players could see where they were on the field. We were in the upper level, and it was snowing so hard, we could hardly see the field. It seemed the solution would be to look at the Jumbotron, but then we were looking through double the snow ... it was a total white out.

As the Chiefs continued to blow the Broncos away, basically only Chiefs fans were left in the stadium, and there were plenty of us to cheer when Marcus scored his 100th touchdown in the snow. I love seeing that clip over and over, knowing that I was there for that. By the end of the game, the Chiefs players were having as much fan as the fans. We saw John Alt, and several other players sliding around the field and making snow angels like kids ... it was a great experience. Our experience didn't end with the game, however.

We loaded the bus, and stopped to eat before heading out on I-70. No one had anticipated how that dinner stop would affect the rest of the trip. The wind picked up, and it continued to snow ... and snow ... and snow ... and snow. It was truly a white out. We were sitting in the first seat behind the bus driver, and you really could not see the road. To add to the excitement, the driver was unable to keep his cool. He was practically standing up, white-knuckled, grasping the steering wheel, all the time exclaiming to all the frightened passengers: "I can't see nothin'! I can't see nothin'!" So the head of the tour decided that perhaps we should take a break at a truck stop he spotted. (I suspect he wanted to take the driver in the back and slap him.) When we stopped, the wind was blowing so hard we could hardly walk across the parking lot. One man stepped off the bus, and literally had his glasses blown right off his face ... never to be found.

After our pit stop, we boarded the bus again, and the tour guide drove the rest of the way, with the bus driver standing up front, still wide-eyed. It took us an EXTRA six hours to get home. We were told after our safe arrival in Kansas City, though, that there were blizzard conditions and they had actually closed I-70 right behind us. Luckily we made it home safely, with a great Chiefs story to tell for the rest of our lives. The football Gods had taken good care of the loyal Chiefs fans.

**- SANDY HUDSON**

**Originally from St. Louis, this transported Kansas City resident is an original member of the Chiefs Geeks, a group of fans who follow Chiefs players at their weekly remote radio shows.**

\* \* \*

Back in 1991, we had been to a Chiefs game a week earlier and noticed all the tailgaters. The next week we were attending another home game and decided to tailgate this time. On the way out of town, we stopped by my parents' house who were not at home at the time and picked up a small grill, charcoal, and lighter fluid. We loaded up and headed to Arrowhead, pulled into the parking lot and set up the grill. After we poured the lighter fluid on the charcoals, lit it and waited for the coals to get hot, we noticed that the coals were not warming up so we poured more lighter fluid on it and waited again. After another 20 minutes, the coals went out with no heat. My good friend "Little Ricky" said, "Stand back you idiots, you don't know what the heck you're doing." He proceeded to pour more lighter fluid on the coals and lit it, all the time he was blowing on the coals to get them going. He ran out of breath finally with no luck. Some friendly tailgaters noticed we were having difficulty lighting the coals and asked us if we would like to use some of their charcoal. We accepted their offer, lit the coals again and we finally had hot coals and ate.

Well, after the game I called my folks but my dad wasn't home at the time and I told my mother the story and to pass on to dad the next time he bought charcoal to please buy a dependable brand as the charcoal he had was terrible. She said she would pass it on and did. The next day dad called and said he understood we had some trouble with the charcoal and I proceeded to reprimand him for buying the cheap stuff. He laughed and said, "Well you big dummy, didn't you read the bag?" I said what for, charcoal is charcoal.

He said, "Well you dumb $&*# if you would have read the bag you would have noticed that the charcoal brickets were for a gas grill and they don't burn!"

Boy, did I feel like a rookie tailgater.

**- MIKE FROM EMPORIA**
**A rookie tailgater.**

\* \* \*

As a Kansas City Chiefs super-fan, I am often asked three questions. What is your most memorable experience as a Chiefs fan? It is not my best memory but it left an indelible mark on me. December 25, 1971. I was 11 years old. It's Christmas Day and our entire family is home for the holidays. I have an old 12-inch black and white TV in my room with rabbit ear antennas. No one in the entire family cared one bit for football, let alone the Chiefs. Something inside me sparked that year and I learned not only about the game of football but also about a team in nearby Kansas City who had just won the Super Bowl and was going to do it again. As Mom yelled repeatedly for me to come down and eat or I wouldn't get to open my presents, I was busily adjusting the rabbit ears on the old TV. Through the static and constant adjustment, I watched as the greatest game in NFL playoff history played itself out to a tragic end as the Chiefs, MY CHIEFS, fell to the Miami Dolphins in double overtime. I will never forget the emotional ups and downs of that game. Ed Podolak's runs, Jan Stenerud's misses and Garo Yepremian's final kick that ended all the hopes of a repeat Super Bowl appearance. It ruined my Christmas! No presents were able to lift my spirits much to the dismay and un-understanding of my un-football minded family. It was that day that I became a diehard Chiefs devotee, an Ed Podolak fan and a hater of Garo Yepremian and the Miami Dolphins!!

The second question I'm often asked is how the character of WEIRDWOLF started and what's that got to do with the Chiefs? Weirdwolf is the spirit of the WOLF-PACK from old Municipal Stadium, resurrected in Arrowhead. The WOLFPACK was a group of rowdy fans in the 1960s and early 70s, who earned a reputation for being howling loud! So now as the first smoke from the first BBQ on game day rises over the uppermost reaches of Arrowhead Stadium, the transformation begins! Just as a full moon affects the legendary werewolf, so does this first smoke affect me, a mild-mannered Chiefs fan, and turns me into the howling, ranting, cheering WEIRDWOLF? ... Keeper of the WOLFPACK tradition, seeking out the next QB to harass and bring to his knees under the revived WOLFPACK of Arrowhead and the 12th man howl!

The third question I'm asked is how long does it take me to get ready for a game? I'm always ready? ... but in real time, I can be face-painted, suited up and in the Arrowhead parking lot, pumping up the best fans in the NFL, in under two hours.

But being a Chiefs fan is more than just wearing a costume and cheering the NFL's best team. Our family knows this first-hand. My wife and I had our first and only child on May 16, 2003; a boy, whom we named Joe Dakota (Joe MONTANA has already been used, so we went to the next state over) Schmidt. After being checked out, it was found that he had a VSD or in simple terms, a hole between the ventricles of the heart. VSDs sometimes close themselves, but in Joe's case it was going to require open-heart surgery. Unfortunately, we would have to wait about a year to have this done. It is a scary thing to put your child through this. Even though it is a surgery that has a very high success rate, it still comes with the risk that we could lose Joe.

So how does this tie in with the Chiefs fan community? Well, I am a huge Chiefs fan and (was) a regular at the Carl Peterson radio shows. I very rarely miss(ed) a show and had been going since the days of the Tim Grunhard shows. I am known as WEIRDWOLF, and as a result I have come to know Carl, Mitch Holthus and Bob Gretz personally and often visit with them. One of the shows I missed was the week of Joe's surgery, which was done the day before Christmas.

Even though we couldn't be at the show we still took our break from the intensive care unit to go to the car and listen to the show. To our surprise, Bob Gretz mentioned Joe in the broadcast and asked for prayers from the Chiefs community for our son. It really touched us, especially my wife, Sondra. This is not the end of the story, however.

Two weeks after Joe was released from the hospital, we decided to take him to the Carl Peterson show at George Brett's Restaurant. When we entered, everybody greeted us and everyone asked about Joe and wanted to see him, including Carl Peterson, who made a special trip through the crowd after the show just to see Joe. It was a wonderful reception not only from our usual friends but also from people who we had never met before or only knew by sight. To top the evening off, during the broadcast, Bob Gretz was introducing that night's guest, Dante Hall. The intro went something like this: "Tonight, 101 The Fox and the Carl Peterson show welcome one of the smallest but most special players on the Chiefs roster, Dante Hall (applause and cheers) but we also want to welcome an even smaller and even more special guest? ... Baby Weirdwolf, Joe Dakota Schmidt, who just went through successful open heart surgery!" (Even louder applause and cheers? ... at least it seemed that way to Sondra and me.) I held Joe up and tears formed in my eyes even as they do now while I write this.

It was amazing to have the Chiefs community show Joe the same amount of support as they gave to one of the top Chiefs players. That's what makes fans in Kansas City special. This is more than football to this community? ... it is a community that happens to love football and a team, the Chiefs, but at the same time realizes that it is a game and when it comes time to step up does so in every way for whoever that person is!

The fans showed that to Joe and us that night in much the same way they showed it when they cheered for the New York Giants after 9/11. Chiefs fans are the greatest fans on earth and I am lucky, proud and thankful to be a part of this Kansas City Chiefs community!

### - LYNN "WEIRDWOLF" SCHMIDT

**A Parkville, Missouri, resident who was selected as a fan inductee into the Pro Football Hall of Fame in 2002. He has appeared on The Jimmy Kimmel Show and the Best Damned Sports Show.**

\* \* \*

My family had season tickets to the Chiefs during the 1970s, and I remember War Paint running onto the field whenever the Chiefs scored. But my most vivid memories of being a Chiefs fan have come during my military career.

We (795th AG Co., Bethany, Mo.) were in Desert Storm. We were in Saudi out in the middle of nowhere, and we had to pull guard duty the night the Chiefs played Warren Moon and the Houston Oilers. Moon killed us that night by throwing for 4 million yards (okay, maybe 400+). I took the walking patrol shift during the game. For walking patrol shift, we had to walk around the wire to make sure no one ran into it or tried to cut through it. That night it got pretty cold (70) ... well, cold from the 110+ degrees it had been that day. So it sure felt like football weather at 2 or 3 in the morning in the middle of nowhere Saudi. My good friends Arthur

Hickey and Adries Spivey were up listening to the game on the radio, keeping me informed of what was going on when we came in to warm up. That night it really sucked to be a Chiefs fan, especially for us. We were in the middle of nowhere, walking the wire, freezing, and then when we get off the shift to warm up, we listened to Warren Moon light up our Chiefs like there was no tomorrow.

Another story that immediately comes to mind was when we were sitting at the Kansas City airport waiting to fly out to deploy to Bosnia for nine months. The Chiefs were playing a playoff game that afternoon and we were not sure that we were going to be able to see it or even listen to it. But Mother Nature stepped in and we had one heck of an ice storm that cancelled all flights until the next day. So the Army put us up in the Embassy Suites at KCI. We all sat and watched as the Chiefs got beat (because they would not play Rich Gannon that day). Once again, a horrible time to be a Chiefs fan. This time, we were getting ready to leave our families for several months, the Chiefs lost and they gave us no good reason why they didn't play Gannon. The next day, we flew out on Southwest Airlines. Interestingly, Chiefs owner Lamar Hunt was on the plane with us. One of our troops even smacked him up side his head with her bag. (But she did not know who he was.) He just sat there, with his glasses all out of whack from the blow to the head, and highlighted the articles in the paper about how bad of a game the Chiefs played.

Not every memory has been bad, though. My best memory of being a Chiefs fan was after I got back from Desert Storm. Bill Maas gave us tickets to a game, lunch at his bar in Independence, and then we got to walk onto the field before the game. It was very cool being down there and seeing the players up close.

Sure, it sucks to be a Chiefs fan sometimes, but when you're from the Kansas City area, who else is there?

**- DARYL BRANDT**

**A longtime Kansas City area resident who works for the Department of Defense. During his career he has been deployed to Desert Shield/Storm, Haiti, Bosnia and Kosovo.**

\* \* \*

Back in 1997, my wife and I decided to go to River Falls for training camp. Our 16-year-old daughter didn't want to stay at home, so she decided to tag along. We were fortunate to be there for family fun night and the exodus downtown to Bo's & Mine after the workout. As we were sitting at the bar, we struck up a conversation with the bartender. During the conversation, we mentioned that our 16-year-old daughter was back at the motel by herself. He told us to go back and get her because in Wisconsin it was legal for underage children to enter bars in the accompaniment of their parents. I traveled back to the motel and retrieved our daughter and then returned to the bar. The players still had not arrived at that time so our daughter was sitting a few feet from us at the bar.

At this point, I need to describe what our daughter Rachel looked like. She stood about 6-feet tall with long, blonde hair and a very slim build. Did I mention that she was 16 then? As the players started filing in, Rachel caught the eye of none other than Pat Barnes. Of

**❝GET HER OUT OF HERE, SHE'S TOO YOUNG❞** – *sign in a River Falls, Wisconsin, bar frequented by Chiefs fans and players during training camp*

course, Mom was keeping a very watchful eye on what was going on. A few minutes later, Rachel whispered to her mother that Pat wanted to buy her a beer. Not realizing her age, it kind of floored him when he found out. The bartender said that the law prevented anyone but legal guardians from buying beer for minors. He said that if we agreed then Pat could give us the money and we buy the beer. Knowing that Rachel probably wouldn't like it anyway, we agreed. Pat soon moved on and joined a group of players congregating next to the bar. The group included the likes of Elvis Grbac, Rich Gannon, Glen Parker and about 10 others.

An hour passed when Rachel asked where the restrooms were located, and the bartender pointed to the rear of the room. In order to get to them, she would have to walk straight through the group of players still lounging around the bar. As she proceeded to the back of the room she had to excuse herself as she made her way through the group. As each player became aware of her, their eyes popped out, their jaws dropped to the floor and their heads followed her movement through the room. My wife and I watched from the bar, but we couldn't contain ourselves any longer. We were laughing so hard that we almost fell off the bar stools. Pat saw the reactions of his fellow teammates and whispered in Elvis' ear. Elvis looked straight at us, pointed his finger to the wall above the door and said: "GET HER OUT OF HERE, SHE'S TOO YOUNG!!!!!!" At that point my wife and I both lost it.

The night continued and we struck up a conversation with two rookies. They were concerned about being cut before the end of training camp. After watching them at practice, we were certain that would not be the case. We talked to these two individuals for most of the night. It was the beginning of a friendship that continues to this day. The two rookies were Eric Hicks and Eric Warfield. Needless to say, we were proven right.

- MAC McCLELLAN

* * *

Although it happened more than 20 years ago, I remember it as if it happened last week. One of my brightest days as a sports fan took place at Arrowhead Stadium. Not on a chilly November Sunday afternoon when my beloved Chiefs were fighting for a coveted playoff spot in the always-challenging AFC West. But on a summer day, during the off-season, on a morning where my greatest hope was to simply step foot on the beautiful turf of my favorite field.

Trips to Kansas City were not unusual for me during those days. In 1977, at the age of five, doctors repaired a "hole in my heart" at KU Medical Center. Every year or two, I would get check ups, which for me were awesome opportunities for Dad to take me to a Royals game, or even take a tour of a stadium at the Truman Sports Complex.

In 1982, after a summer trip to the Medical Center, plans were for Dad and me to see the Royals play the Texas Rangers, and to possibly tour Royals Stadium for the second time. But tours were shut down early during home games. So we decided, even though it was the off-season, to see if anyone would be willing to take us into the locker room and onto the field at Arrowhead Stadium. What we found was more than a tour. It was a dream for a 10-year-old boy who had never met a professional athlete.

As we walked into Arrowhead, we were told that no tours were available at that time. Disappointed, we began to leave. But as I opened the front door, I heard chatter. Lots of chatter. Then laughs. Then I saw them. The Chiefs. The entire team. Art Still dominated the room, standing so tall to my left near a doorway that would not allow his entry without a duck. I saw Marv Levy, the head coach that we hoped would be the answer to the Chiefs' woes. I saw the great Nick Lowery, Gary Barbaro, wide receiver Henry Marshall, and my favorite player ... Joe Delaney (who the next year would die in a heroic attempt to save some people from drowning). My first thought, after the stunned feeling faded away slightly, was autographs. I sprinted to the car, with dad jogging behind, to find something ... a notebook, a pad, a napkin ... something that I could keep stored away forever. The only thing we could find were two pictures ... small 5x7 pictures ... of my two-year-old sister ... in a baby beauty contest. Perfect.

We took the two pictures back to the complex, and the autograph session was on. Marv Levy started the show, signing the back of the picture after commenting that my sister was "very pretty." Then Barbaro, Marshall, Lowery, Still and the man I remember the most, Joe Delaney. Delaney had just completed a 1,000-yard rushing season, stealing the hearts of many Chiefs fans who had never observed such power and speed. He was my favorite player, and did he deliver on that day. I don't remember much of our conversation, but I remember Delaney spent more time with my father and me than any other player did. He signed the back of my sister's picture, and made my day with his charming personality. Although Joe Delaney played only 23 games for the Kansas City, he will always be my favorite Chief.

The morning ended with a player finding the back window in his car shattered, and many of his teammates looking for the culprit in the parking lot. But there was nothing shattered in my heart. Only thrills for a young fan that had never once met an athlete of that stature. The shattering happened for me months later, when I learned that Delaney drowned while trying to save several young boys who did not know how to swim. That news told me immediately that the time Delaney spent with me was sincere, and he may have enjoyed it as much as I did.

Today, watching the Chiefs on Sunday is ritualistic for a few of us here in Salina. Several things that we do will fit right in with most guys that gather regularly on Sunday afternoons, including the beer intake, making chili or grilling brats, and throwing things at the TV when the game doesn't go just right.

But one ritual that a friend developed during the 2003 season is a bit unusual. It was the final Sunday of September, and Brian, who hosts our Chiefs watch party each Sunday, was showing off his new Chiefs Halloween mask. Also, he purchased an Arrowhead hat that was a take-off of the "Cheeseheads" made popular in Green Bay. By the end of that Sunday, a new ritual was born.

The beer was "goin' down smooooothhhh," as Brian would say. And the Chiefs were winning. They took down the Baltimore Ravens, 17-10, pushing our celebration to a new limit. Brian disappeared, only to emerge out front in the middle of the street, with a Chiefs flag in one hand, an American flag in the other, and the Chiefs mask covering his face, and the Arrowhead hat on top of his head. He took off running, yelling, ranting and raving about the Chiefs' win. From that day on, any Kansas City victory warranted a trip around the block from Brian, fully decked out in his new outfit, whooping and hollering from start to finish. Classic.

The best was after a Chiefs victory over the Broncos the next week. I stayed beerless that day, and Brian decided a trip on foot around the block would not be enough. So we jumped in my Ford Escape, flags and costume included, and honked our way throughout the neighborhood. We found a truck just one block away decorated in Broncos stickers. We stopped, honked for a minute or so, and Brian gave the home "the bird" before our departure.

Any Chiefs fans are welcome to join our Sunday Chiefs watch party. Just stop off on Kenison Street in Salina on game day, and be ready for a riot. Brian never fails to deliver!

By the way, even though I'm not a regular at Arrowhead on Sundays, and I didn't get to tour the facility on that day in 1982, my day to walk on the stadium's turf happened 21 years later. As the radio sideline reporter of the Kansas State football team, I worked two games at Arrowhead in 2003. The Wildcats played USC to open the season, and returned to beat the No. 1-ranked Oklahoma Sooners in the Big XII Championship game. But no trip to Arrowhead will ever top that summer day in 1982 when a father and his son just hoped for a tour of their favorite stadium, but instead made lifetime memories by meeting the great players and people who were the Kansas City Chiefs.

- CHRIS ALLISON
**Sports director for six radio stations in central Kansas.**

I was a 23-year season ticket holder and follow the Chiefs as much as anyone. I was born and raised in the Kansas City area, so I became a Chiefs fan in the late 1960s, when I was four or five years old, and have not looked back. Initially, I became a fan because they were my hometown team, but now I can't imagine cheering for anybody else.

There have been so many fantastic memories as a Chiefs fan. First of all, October 2003, when the Chiefs were playing the Raiders in Oakland on Monday Night Football. My children wanted to wear their Chiefs clothing that day just like me. I wore my Chiefs polo shirt to work, my daughter wore her Tony Gonzalez jersey to school and my 18-month-old son was in his Chiefs toddler outfit. (The daycare provider thought it was cute how all of us dressed alike for the game. She had never seen anything like that living in Phoenix all of her life.) I also remember the year, while working in the Kansas City area, we gave the Chiefs' coaching staff a decorated "horse shoe" to hang in the locker room for good luck. We gave it to them at the 1993 Kickoff Luncheon. Coach Marty Schottenheimer remarked during his speech to the luncheon crowd that he had been passed this gift of a horse shoe, and he was very appreciative of the gift. He thanked us publicly and told the audience that the horse shoe would be hung in a prominent location. The idea came from my wife's grandparents, who used to do the same thing for the University of Kansas back in the 1940s and '50s. The horse shoes came from horses off their ranch southeast of Lawrence, KS.

One of my earliest memories of being a Chiefs fan happened when I was a kid. We attended a Chiefs-Raiders game, and sat in the bleachers in left field of old

Municipal Stadium. I couldn't see the field very well because I was only about five years old, but I remember looking up in the sky and seeing a crop duster writing: GO CHIEFS. It's a vision that hasn't left my memory.

The first game I attended at Arrowhead Stadium was a Monday Night game against the Chicago Bears in 1973. My dad and I rode the bus to the game and our seats were on the lower level, about the 30-yard line, behind the Bears sideline. I remember looking around from that view and thinking how awesome it was.

Not every experience has been great, though. I remember the day the news was announced that Joe Delaney had drowned attempting to rescue those boys in the pond, and when they announced that Mike Bell had been arrested for drug abuse. I thought this couldn't be happening to a Kansas City player. Of course, it was and it meant we were now no different than other professional sports franchises. Another of the dark days for Chiefs fans was learning that Derrick Thomas had been seriously injured in an automobile accident. We had flown from Kansas City to Phoenix that Sunday morning in January for a belated Christmas holiday with my in-laws in the Phoenix area. We flew out of KCI around 9:00 that morning and were not aware of any snow in the forecast. That Sunday night at the in-laws' home, we were channel surfing when we saw ESPN talking about Derrick Thomas, unaware of anything . My wife and I just looked at each other, trying to figure out what snow-covered roads they could be talking about. I went up to the in-laws' computer and viewed several Kansas City websites only to confirm that DT's accident had occurred, along with many other serious accidents on snow-covered roadways. Unfortunately, Derrick passed away several weeks later. We moved to Phoenix six weeks later.

D.T. provided Chiefs fans with some incredible games. I'll never forget that game on October 4, 1999, when the Chiefs were playing the Seattle Seahawks on the ESPN Sunday night game. You know the story – bad weather around Kansas City all weekend, very heavy rain. During the tailgate party time, three hours prior to kick-off, it did nothing more than just sprinkle. However, some 25 minutes into the game, the skies opened up like this stadium had only seen once before. Rain water was cascading down the stairs and out onto the field. We all remember the picture of Derrick Thomas kneeling down, drenched in his somewhat off-white pants, waterlogged, dark red jersey, and water a couple of inches deep around his legs.

I sat through that entire game with two women, one of them my wife. Of course we were ushered to the concourse area because of a tornado threat midway through the second quarter. Until that time, our feet had remained relatively dry. When they announced that a couple of the parking lot exits were closed because of high water just shortly after the start of the second half, I was sure the Little Blue River was flooding. Getting home would be an issue. However, the women and I decided to stay through the game, and even more rain. When it was all said and done, I told those women that if they could make it through this game with these weather conditions, they should be able to survive anything else we could possibly endure at a Chiefs game.

But my biggest memory of being a Chiefs fan happened several years earlier. For my 13th birthday, my parents bought me two season tickets for the 1977 season, for my father and me to attend. (I guess they got the idea from my persistence in listening to and/or watching every game for the years prior.)

A couple of years after we got those tickets, my father was diagnosed with terminal brain cancer. He continued to try to attend the games as weather and health would allow after surgery and chemotherapy. Labor Day weekend 1979, my father was readmitted to the hospital because it was obvious his time was short. He slipped into a coma. That Sunday, the first weekend of the NFL season, was to begin and the Colts were in town to face the Chiefs. The family urged me to go and to see the game, because at that point in time there was nothing I could do by sitting around the hospital room. So I went with a very good friend of mine, Doug Scheibe. The Chiefs scored two touchdowns on the very same type of play, and beat the Colts 14-0.

When Doug and I returned to the bus stop to be picked up, my family was there and what I feared had happened to my father had happened. He passed away during the game. I held on to those season tickets through college, marriage and the birth of my first child. Every once in a while during one of those games in that 21-year span, I could hear Dad's voice yelling out at something the Chiefs had done and I would instinctively turn around only to find him not there. In the years that followed, I moved my tickets to sit with my best friend, Mark LaRue, and his father.

I now live in Mesa, Arizona, and follow the Chiefs as much as I ever had or possibly can. I transferred the season tickets to my best friend's father and his family, because he was a grandfather and both of his grandsons were beginning to show an interest in football and the

Chiefs. Whenever I'm back in Kansas City and the Chiefs are at home, I make plans to attend.

Being able to attend games with my father prior to his illness and death, and then attending games with my wife some 15 years later, are great memories for me. Now, my wife, who used to be a Broncos fan, and I are cheering on the Chiefs from some 1,500 miles away, with my children right by my side.

Not long ago, my wife asked me about our move to the Phoenix area. I told her I enjoy it here but that DirecTV and the Internet make it even more enjoyable. In other words, I don't miss a play or any news about the Chiefs. It's not tough being a fan of the Chiefs, or any other team, here in Arizona especially because the Cardinals stink as an organization. But the Internet and the dish availability of the games on Sunday make it seem as if I never left K.C.

**- STEVE HALL**

**A Kansas City Chiefs fan who lives in Mesa, Arizona, and is married to a Broncos fan.**

\* \* \*

I have been a Chiefs fan since the year that they moved here from Dallas. The second year that they were in Kansas City, my dad bought season tickets, and I was hooked. I met several of the Chiefs players when I was about eight years old. My dad was a reporter for KCKN radio in Kansas City, and I got to go to the locker room with him after a couple of games. What an experience!

A few of my favorite players (and this is not because I have seen some of them naked) are Otis Taylor, Chris Burford, Willie Lanier, Jerry Mays, Aaron Brown,

Jimmy Marsalis, and Johnny Robinson. Really, almost all of the old-school Chiefs plus players like Art Still, Gary Spani, Gary Barbaro, Deron Cherry and Tim Grunhard.

I still remember my first few games at Arrowhead because of the people that sat in front of us. The wife had one favorite phrase – go Chiefies! And the husband had his own exclamation – run two, pass, kick – to show his frustration with the predictability of the offense.

My worst memory? Two words: Lin Elliott.

Several memories stand out through the years. One year, the Chiefs were playing the San Diego Chargers on Monday Night Football, when Tamarick Vanover returned a kick for a touchdown. (I believe it was in overtime, but at the very least at the end of the game.) Being 6-foot-5, I should know better, but I was so excited that I jumped out of my chair with my fists raised in triumph, and promptly broke my hand on the ceiling of my home.

Sadly, the second story ends the same way, with a broken hand, when James Hasty returned an interception for a touchdown against the Raiders. I'm a slow learner I guess.

Another story that stands out is from the Christmas Day game in '71 (the longest game in NFL history). My father had given up his tickets to the game so that he could spend Christmas with the family. I was 12 years old, and we listened to the game on the radio. My father and uncle tried to tune in channel 27 out of Topeka to watch the game. Since this was before cable, the reception, in my opinion, was non-existent. My father and uncle swore that they could see the game, but all that anyone else saw was snow. I can still remember them yelling at Jan Stenerud for "clearly" missing the field goals.

My final memory has to do with old Municipal Stadium and my standing in the family. I am the youngest of six children, so I always got the hand-me-downs, even when it came to Chiefs tickets. My dad had four season tickets, but two went to my uncle because they split the cost. Needless to say, the only chances that I ever had to go to the games were during the worst weather. In the old stadium, there were I-beams that supported the second level, with a drainage pipe that ran down the side of the beam and deposited any water at the feet of the person sitting next to the beam (me). I must have been 10 years old when I got the chance to go to a miserable game. I can't even remember who we played because there was freezing rain, snow and sleet the whole game. I thought that my mom prepared me well (two pairs of socks covered by a plastic bag and another pair of socks, followed by tennis shoes and galoshes), but when we finally got home, my parents discovered that my toes had a mild case of frostbite. I'll never remember the game, but I'll never forget the day.

**- STORMY FLOYD**
**A Blue Springs, Missouri, resident whose son Brandon was a standout wide receiver at Blue Springs High School.**

\* \* \*

I took a road trip to Green Bay during the 2003 season with two of my cousins and one of my best friends. We purchased our tickets on E-Bay, and sat four rows off the field in the end zone where Eddie Kennison caught the game-winning pass. The end zone was a hush except for the few Chiefs fans; we were still going nuts when the team was walking off the field. Johnnie Morton jumped into us, we were getting high-fived and such. It was the best afternoon and one of my best-ever road trips.

The trip was made complete the next morning when, on our way out of town, we filled up the car with gas. I bought a couple of different newspapers to read during the drive home. When I got in the van, I handed the Milwaukee paper to Sherry. All of the sudden, she slammed me in the chest and screamed "Oh my GOD – LOOK!!" There, on the front page of the sports section, was a picture of the Kennison catch. The crowd behind him was a blur except for four Chiefs jerseys, arms in the air, mouths wide open. IT WAS US!

What was even better was there was this obnoxious woman sitting in front of us that kept waving a Packer towel in our face during the game. The look of disappointment on her face in the newspaper photo was just as priceless as seeing ourselves in that picture!

- KAREN MEDLEY
A Chiefs fan for life.

\* \* \*

As long as I can remember, my mom (Donna) and dad (John), who are season-ticket holders, have rarely missed a home game since the Chiefs moved to Kansas City. Because of them, I've been a Chiefs fan all of my life. I am fortunate enough to say that I attended the longest football game in history because my older sister got sick, and I got to go in default. My first Chiefs game was earlier that same year when they played the Chargers at Municipal Stadium on my sixth birthday.

My family grew up with the Chiefs in good times and bad. We meet every Sunday at the home games to tailgate. My Dad is the biggest die-hard fan I've ever met. I've never seen a guy get so excited about watching/scouting the third team players in the pre-season. The family joke is how excited our dad gets when the Chiefs play. No matter how badly they play, he'll always watch every play. I remember watching games in the late 1970s and early '80s, when the team stunk. But we would stay at the stadium until the last play.

Dad's favorite story is when the Chiefs won Super Bowl IV. There was a tropical storm before the game and the stadium was outdoors, unlike the Superdome. After the game, Dad was walking back to his car across a 2'x12' plank that went over some mud. A belligerent Viking fan was coming the other way against the traffic and was pushing his way across the Chiefs fans. Dad shoved the guy off the board and he fell into the mud to the delight of the other Chiefs fans.

My most surreal memory is the game in which Bo Jackson came back to Kansas City as a Raider and the fans threw baseballs at him. I remember Raider linebacker Matt Millen launching a ball back into the crowd.

But one of the best times I had was in 1998 when I was hosting three karate students from Tokyo, Japan. Our sister karate club in Japan always participated in a student exchange. That year, the students arrived in Dallas and then went to Oklahoma for a week. Then they traveled to Kansas City and finally went on to Denver. I picked the Japanese up at the Oklahoma border and drove them to Kansas City. In conversations on the way, I found out that they were all Dallas Cowboys fans. They knew who Troy Aikman, Emmitt

Smith and Michael Irvin were, but they didn't know a single Chief.

Eventually, we made it to Kansas City, where my friends and I proceeded to show them the town. The Japanese were wearing "letter jackets" from their Tokyo karate club that night. We stopped by Kelly's in Westport. Once inside, I noticed Derrick Thomas and his entourage enjoying the night by the bar. I pointed out to my guests who Derrick Thomas was and explained to them his status in Kansas City. It just so happened that there was a local newspaper stand over by the doorway with a picture of Derrick on the cover. Our guests conversed with each other in Japanese and then turned to ask me if Derrick Thomas was the team captain. After I told them yes, they asked me if they could take a picture with him. I went over to the entourage and tried to ask Derrick. The entourage was a little protective of him and it took a little bit of work to get through to him. When I told him the request of our Japanese guests, he graciously posed for pictures with them. I later found out that this was the highlight of their trip to America.

The best part of the story is what happened later. On Saturday, I passed our Japanese guests off to friends who lived in Denver. That Sunday, the Japanese and Denver people were watching the Broncos vs. Chiefs game at a pro-Broncos drinking establishment. I only wished I could have seen the looks on the Broncos fans when the Japanese students went crazy when Derrick got his 100th career sack during that game. My Denver friends called me that night to ask me how I had brain-washed the Japanese with the Chiefs in such a short time.

Really, though, how much brainwashing does it take to turn a Broncos' fan into a Chiefs' fan?

**- DAVID MARTIN**

**Played football at Shawnee Mission South and was the back-up to future NFL player Rodney Peete in 1983.**

\* \* \*

In 2003, I was inducted into the Pro Football Hall of Fame in Canton, Ohio, as the ultimate Chiefs fan in a contest called the Visa Hall of Fans. My ultimate goal is to reach as many people as possible with the message that the Chiefs family is the greatest family in the world and as a family, together we will make the U.S. a much greater place to live though all of our efforts.

Through all of my research I believe I'm only one of five people from the state of Kansas to be in the Hall of Fame. The other four are players. There is no way I can explain the excitement around this whole event. To be acknowledged as one of the greatest Chiefs fans ever is unexplainable. In attendance at Canton were all of my family and my best friends to share in the event. In attendance also were two of my best friends that had recently passed away. I paid respect to them in front of all 80,000 there, by having a moment with them. To see how overwhelmed my friends and family were by the whole event is priceless.

I was selected for the Hall of Fame based on the following letter:

*To start off there is no bigger Chiefs fan than me. I bleed straight red and yellow. I have been a Chiefs fan all of my 28 years on this earth. I have never missed a game, either watching it live from Arrowhead, on TV or on the* radio. *My knowledge of my team is matched by very few and my loyalty is clearly visible with the two Chiefs tattoos, one on each arm. I also average at least four hours a day researching stats, chatting Chiefs or talking on the phone. This is my eleventh year of going to every home game. My round trip now is only 4 hours, but it has been 10, and up to 14 hours during that period. I used to go to games just in shorts and slippers and paint my whole body red and yellow. For three years I also dressed up in a yellow and red Spiderman costume for Andre Rison. In 2001 I created a new character called XFACTOR which stands for external factors such as weather elements, coaching, players, injuries, etc. I represent the greatest XFACTOR: all 79,000-plus fans at Arrowhead and the millions watching at home. In other words, I represent the 12th man. I wear a spandex costume completely covered in Chiefs garb. At the games I'm always being put on the Jumbotron raising the whole stadium on all crucial defensive downs. I have a car that proudly displays the love for my team which is covered with 10 Chiefs magnets and 7 different lettering displays on it. I have a Chiefs Fan Club website, which celebrates Chiefs fans. I average about 160 pictures each game just on my camera; with fellow Chiefs fans there's no way to count how many pictures actually have been taken of me. I do a lot of appearances and charity events. I also make appearances at schools, hospitals, and handicapped facilities, sharing my excitement about the Chiefs. My whole goal is to help the team, help make life miserable for opposing teams, excite fellow Chiefs fans, and to bridge the gap with the children so someday they will continue the rich tradition of the Chiefs.*

This all started 29 years ago with my dad who is the biggest Chiefs fan. My parents divorced at a very young age so I spent only Sundays with my dad. On Sundays it was always Chiefs football and then fishing. My first memory was that dad used to take me fishing, which I wanted to do, but Dad would not leave until after the Chiefs game. So, we sat and watched, without fail. In 1993, when I went to college, I met a buddy that had two season tickets to Arrowhead so I started going to every game with him. This is when everything began.

My dad was seven hours away and we could no longer watch the games together. So, I decided that I was going to paint my body half red and half yellow, wear only Chiefs shorts, socks, slippers and a red wig so I could get on TV and my dad back home could see his son and be proud. I never made it on TV doing this but I found something else very important. By doing this I raised everyone's excitement to a different level. I have transformed over the years from that first "costume" to Spiderman, to Chiefman, and now to XFACTOR. I have found that I raise the excitement level for all Chiefs fans, I bridge the gap for the next generation of Chiefs fans with all the kid events that I do, and I symbolize everything that is good about the Chiefs.

At my all-school reunion in 2000, my classmates convinced me to do my Spiderman act at the fairgrounds. I was no longer Spiderman due to Rison being cut a few months earlier, but the character still had a mystique that my classmates knew all about. I agreed and went to the fairgrounds in my hometown as Spiderman. I made an appearance and signed autographs and took many pictures. The next thing I know, I'm doing the stuff that I did at Arrowhead for a couple of years. I climbed on top on the 4-H building and started a Chiefs pep rally. I led everyone in singing Chiefs songs and displayed my Spiderman moves in front of everyone. The police became aware of my activities and yelled at me to get down. I did just as they instructed, and jumped off about a 15-foot building, onto concrete, in Chiefs slippers. As one might guess, I ended up with two sprained ankles and a broken right middle toe.

After Andre Rison got cut and the year before I became XFACTOR I came up with the idea of Chiefsman. I painted my body and had a lady sew me a vertical red and yellow spandex body suit. I then completed the outfit by adding Chiefs socks, shorts, slippers, wrist bands, gloves, a yellow wig and my Chiefs foam Arrowhead hat. This was a big hit with everyone, especially the kids. I, however, was not a Chiefs superhero but rather I resembled that famous guy from McDonalds. Yes, I looked exactly like Ronald McDonald. This outfit, however, is the shell of XFACTOR now with some definite upgrades. This was a very humbling experience but now is something that my friends and I get a big laugh about.

Because of all of the events that I do, I make four costumes a year now due to them getting worn out. I make three yellow and red ones and one red and white away outfit. It takes me about 45 minutes to completely put on the costume, but it's well worth it because I spend about 12 hours each game day at Arrowhead. My 2004 outfits have at least 35 Chiefs patches sewn on each one with the main one having 43. I get these from buying old Chiefs shirts and cutting them out and sewing on the costumes. Each costume costs about $350 to completely make, not including the cost of the Chiefs garb I put on top of it.

A couple of years ago I sponsored my own bowling team. Our team wore my XFACTOR T-shirts that I make every year. They have XFACTOR on the front and they say Chiefs Fans Are The Greatest – XFACTOR on the back. Briar was a Raiders fan and didn't enjoy wearing these shirts, so one Sunday night he showed up in an XFACTOR shirt that was black and silver and said Raiders Fans Are The Greatest – XFACTOR. He went to where I got my shirts done and told them that I wanted them to make this shirt. Bowling was on Sunday nights, so a few times I drove straight to bowling after a game and bowled in my XFACTOR costume. On one of these nights I was a little upset that the Chiefs had lost, and the shirt that Briar wore only rubbed in my frustration. So, I bet him that whoever had the highest bowling score the next game could dress up the other the next week and would have to go bowling in the other's outfit. I bowled about a 190 game and beat him by 80 pins. Needless to say, he had to wear my complete XFACTOR costume the next week. Ultimate payback for changing my shirt. I can't wait until he gets married, because it will give me a great chance to break out those pictures.

I've had some incredible moments as a recognizable fan. After the Raiders game in 2003, I took a group of my friends, a few who had never been to a Chiefs game, to get autographs at the players' parking lot. A friend that sits in my section happened to be over there also. We got a few autographs and he said here comes Greg Robinson getting into his car. He kept saying, over and over, let's get Greg's autograph. Finally, the car pulled to the gate and I led the group over to the car. I turned around and

Greg signed my cape. I turned around and said, "Thank you, Greg." As soon as I said it I realized my blunder. But it was too late. He simply said: My name is Al. Yes, Al Saunders, the greatest offensive coordinator in the league, just got called Greg by one of the greatest fans in the league. It was a perfect Southwest Airlines' Gotta Get Away commercial moment.

Another time I was around the players' parking lot, the December game against the Steelers, a couple of months before Derrick Thomas passed away, I was doing my Spiderman act for a bunch of fans. Somebody yelled out, Hey, Spiderman, someone wants to talk to you. And he pointed at a car pulling into the players' parking lot. I walked over to the vehicle and bent over to see who it was. Once I saw that unbelievable smile, I knew that it was none other than the greatest football player of all-time, Derrick Thomas. He told me that it was an important day and that I needed to kick ass that day. I had a hard time speaking but I told him that was his job. He said, "You don't know how much of a difference you guys make." He also said that it was because of fans like us that he would retire as a Chief. We told each other to go kick some ass, and that was it. No one can ever take away my last moment with DT.

Another story that pops into my mind happened during halftime of a 2002 game when I left my seat to go use the restroom. As usual, as soon as I hit the aisle, I had people approach me wanting to take a picture with me. After a few pictures a lady approached me, and I assumed that she wanted a picture, so I put my arm on her shoulder. She said, "What are you doing?" Then she added, "You are a moron." I asked nicely what she was talking about and she said, "Didn't you hear the announcement before the game that said please abstain from constant standing?" I said, "Yes, but I don't stand always; just on defensive downs." I asked her where she was sitting and I'd try to accommodate her. She responded that she was about 20 rows above me. I said, "Well, I'm a tall guy, about 6-1, but I know that I couldn't possibly be obstructing your view." She then again said, "You just don't understand, you moron. Every time they put you on the Jumbotron, instructing everyone to stand up and go crazy, everyone stands up and I can't see the game." All I could do was laugh at the lady and walk away. Must have been the opposing team's fan.

**- TY ROWTON**
**X-Factor, who was inducted into the fans' wing of the Pro Football Hall of Fame in 2003.**

\* \* \*

**M**y brother and I were waiting outside the players' entrance at Municipal Stadium after a Kansas City A's game in the mid-1960s. We were pretty knowledgeable, even though we were only six and eight years old. We knew we would recognize the A's when they came out, so we waited to get some autographs. We were the only two there, besides our parents, who were waiting in the car. A black man came out of the locker room, and though we thought he looked familiar, we couldn't figure out who he was. We asked him for his autograph anyway, because we knew he was "somebody." He told us that he was not a baseball player, so we turned and walked back to the door. A car pulled up and someone in the car said, "C'mon Otis, sign for them." We then realized the familiar face was Chiefs receiver Otis Taylor. He "ran" from us but we caught him up the sidewalk a bit, and he gladly signed autographs for us.

We were part of the Chiefs Huddle Club in 1968. Late in the season, the Chiefs opened practice for kids who were in the Huddle Club and their families. After watching practice, we roamed the stands and collected autographs from the players stationed at various points. Mike Garrett, one of my favorites, was standing in front of one of the seats, facing the crowd, which was above him. My dad was standing in the chair in the row closer to the field (behind Mike's back). My dad lost his balance and let out a yell. In one motion, Mike turned around and caught Dad from falling several feet backwards and probably getting hurt. Mike then turned and signed more autographs as if nothing had happened.

**- DAVID SMALE**
**Kansas City-based sports writer.**

\* \* \*

It was dark in the wee hours of a Sunday morning in the fall of 1987. Actually, as a college student it might be more accurate to say it was very late at night. My girlfriend (who later became my wife) and I made the trek to the loading dock of McCain Auditorium on the campus of Kansas State University. Along with more than 200 other members of the "Pride of Wildcat Land" marching band, we retrieved our instruments from the building, and loaded them and ourselves onto a charter bus to make our annual trip to Kansas City to perform at a Chiefs game. It would be a long day, but one I always looked forward to.

I had been to Arrowhead several times as a kid. My parents and some of their friends had season tickets for several years. So, once or twice a year, when one of the other couples could not go, my brother and I would use their tickets. The tickets were always in the end zone under the original scoreboard in the upper deck. However, this particular day would be my fourth trip to a game as a member of the K-State Marching Band.

The visiting band would always sit in the first few rows of the end zone seats. Honestly, the view wasn't too great except when the teams got well into our end of the field. But these trips didn't cost me a penny, so I never complained. The Chiefs organization always treated us very well and they would feed us a box lunch after we rehearsed in the morning, before our pre-game performance.

During our rehearsals we were always admonished to "stay out of the end zones." They didn't want us messing up the nice paint job so it would look good on television. But the rehearsal time was usually interesting. In those early hours of a game day there was plenty of activity at the stadium. It was not unusual to see the TV announcers talking to somebody or recording a piece for the broadcast. The Chiefs' cheerleaders would often be stretching and lightly preparing for the day. Occasionally, even a player would be out on the field very early for one reason or another. But it was all very casual and relaxed, yet in anticipation of 78,000 visitors and NFL football.

That particular year the trip to the Chiefs game was late in the fall and was our last marching band event of the season. I no longer remember the opponent, nor the outcome of the game. The drama of that day came after the game. Dave, one of the other trombonists, decided to celebrate the end of his collegiate marching band career by trashing the old trombone he marched with throughout college. He invited my girlfriend and I to join him in his celebration.

The location of the festivities was the parking lot by our busses just outside the tunnel at Arrowhead. That was a fun place to be because the players parked out there and often we would still be there when they would leave the stadium. Other fans would walk around there to get autographs and see their favorite players.

Dave directed the demise of his trombone. We began by knocking some dents in it and we beat it around a little bit. Then Dave decided to destroy the "slide" (the moving part of the instrument that allows you to play different notes). We each grabbed hold of the slide and Dave counted to three. The three of us tugged in opposite directions. Quickly, it broke apart. It was oddly brittle for metal. It seemed to almost splinter as it gave way. I heard a bit of a scream come from the direction of my girlfriend. Dave and I looked toward her and found her holding her bleeding hand. The slide had busted right where she was holding it and impaled her palm. She was bleeding quite extensively and the stadium staff suggested we go to the ambulance that is always parked in the tunnel during the games. Fortunately, it was still there and they were willing to assist her. The EMT slowed the bleeding, cleaned the wound, and put a butterfly (bandage) on her hand. Being a good boyfriend, I accompanied my future wife during her ordeal. As I watched the guy clean her wound and watched her flinch as he did it, I began to sweat. My head began to spin, I felt nauseous and my vision started to dim. My "knight in shining armor" routine was quickly falling flat (quite literally) as I nearly passed out from the experience. My girlfriend and the EMT noticed I was looking more than just a little pale and suggested that I lie down on the concrete tunnel floor while the EMT cooled me off with a wet towel. My girlfriend found this quite humorous, so I guess I did help her through her ordeal, though not in the noble way I had planned!

After my girlfriend's hand was mended and I was able to stand up and walk, we made the journey back through the tunnel to our bus. A short time later we left the parking lot and made the trip back to Manhattan and the loading dock at McCain Auditorium.

To this day, Leona has a faint scar on the palm of her hand and I have a faint scar in my pride from that Sunday afternoon at Arrowhead Stadium.

**- JEFF ARMSTRONG**
**City planner for Abilene, Kansas.**

\* \* \*

Go KC! That simple phrase embodies how my buddies and I have felt about the Chiefs and the NFL since we were able to understand football. My friends and I have been die-hard Chiefs fans for quite some time. We loved the days when Deron Cherry roamed the secondary, put up with the offense when they ran on 1st, 2nd, & 3rd downs during Marty-ball, and then celebrated being able to see the highest flying offense in the NFL.

But one of our biggest memories came from a game when our picture found its way to the front page of The Topeka Capital Journal, our hometown newspaper, on Friday October 18, 1996. We were at a Thursday night game against the Seattle Seahawks. The Chiefs dominated all three phases of the game and cruised to a 34-16 victory.

At that time, we were only 16 years old, so that October 17 seemed like the longest school day of the year. I was lucky enough to have a grandma that had season tickets since 1990, so I had been to many Chiefs games. My three buddies had been to only a couple of games apiece before that game, so it made this picture even more special. We were all from Shawnee Heights High School and this game was during our junior year.

> **" Oops ... he recognized his player in that photograph. Without a shirt. The one who missed practice the day before because of a 'doctor's appointment.' "**
> — *RYAN SMITH, a "wayward" high school football player who lives in Topeka, Kansas*

We planned on leaving at 3:00 that afternoon, right after school. This worked for Taylor Ewing (the G), Austin Hamm (the O), and Jared Richert (the C), but for me (the K), there was a dilemma. It was the middle of our high school football season, so to see the Chiefs game meant that I would have to skip practice. I braved it, told a coach I had a doctor's appointment and stuck to the plan.

As we were getting on Interstate-70 to make the drive to Arrowhead, we pulled alongside Mrs. Henson, our math teacher, in the toll booth lane next to us. After passing the hottest teacher at Shawnee Heights, we knew we were in for an exciting night. We had planned on painting our chests for the game two weeks before, when I received the fourth row tickets from my father's company. However, we didn't know that it was going to be 35 degrees. After debating about it in the parking lot, we decided to fight the cold, and started painting each other's chests. We went to our seats on the 15-yard line about 45 minutes before game time. We later found out that a picture of us was taken during pregame. We stood and cheered and made friends with everyone around us for the whole game. It was a great time.

We had a game the next night back in Topeka at Shawnee Heights. Every Friday morning we had a pre-school meeting at 7:00 in the locker room. That morning I rushed into the meeting, sat down and saw a couple of funny looks coming in my direction. A few moments later, the coach walked in with a copy of that morning's paper, congratulated my teammates who had listened to his instructions about staying bundled and warm when outside, and then gave me a look of disappointment. Oops? ... he recognized his player in that photograph. Without a shirt. The one who missed practice the day before because of a "doctor's appointment." After the meeting, I ran to meet my friends. They had not yet seen a paper that morning, but lucky for us, the picture was plastered in every hallway and around every corner we turned. That picture got me a reserved seat on the sideline for the game that night, but it also gave my friends and me a memory embracing our passion for the Chiefs and the enjoyment we had together.

- **Ryan Smith**
**Who lives in Topeka, Kansas.**

# Mr. Music

Mr. Music is Tony DiPardo, the now 97-year-old former bandleader of the Kansas City Chiefs. He worked 55 years on a handshake agreement with team founder Lamar Hunt.

This section recalls a special moment ... and a very special friendship.

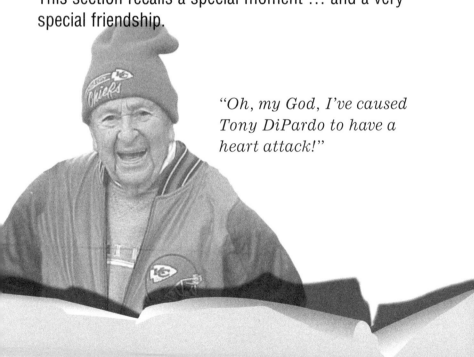

*"Oh, my God, I've caused Tony DiPardo to have a heart attack!"*

# 'That's the Greatest Return I Have Ever Seen in My Life'

He'd appeared on *Late Night with David Letterman,* and would later hit the streets of New York City with Jay Z, signing autographs for fans who had watched him star in NFL stadiums across the country.

Dante Hall had earned a super hero's nickname, a spot on Letterman's couch next to Pam Anderson, and the undying respect of his coaches, teammates and Chiefs fans.

He was nicknamed the "X-Factor" because there were so many ways he could help the Chiefs claim a victory. While he provided a lifetime of memories in just a seven-year stay in Kansas City, the most memorable came on a heart-stopping punt return against the Denver Broncos in 2003.

"People still talk about that return," Hall said, "and I love 'em for asking. I know I'll never forget it."

Micah Knorr's punt was sailing to him.

"I think I caught it near the 7. It was a booboo play. It should have been a fair catch. The coaches tell me to be smart and the first part of that return was not smart. I think I caught it on the 7, went back to the 5, then to the 2 and back even farther. I just kept getting dumber and dumber and dumber. I thought, 'Oh, I've got to get out of this jam.'"

He did. For the fourth week in a row, the Chiefs' mighty mite returned a kick for a touchdown. Hall juked two defenders inside the 5, darted past three more

> **"I think I caught it near the 7. It was a booboo play. It should have been a fair catch."**
> — Dante Hall, describing the first few seconds of his miracle punt return against Denver.

between the 5 and 15, and then let Mike Maslowski block Knorr into the cheap seats to create a wide open field.

"People have heard me say that Dante would return a kick for a touchdown when everything doesn't go perfectly," coach Dick Vermeil said. "Maybe this was the return."

Maslowski, who earned a starting role for the Chiefs because of his aggressive play on special teams, added, "When it comes down to the punter, you can bet Dante's going to score. I look up and there are five or six guys ready to tackle him, and then you see him take off and he's going for another touchdown. I don't know how he does it."

ESPN analyst and former Chiefs quarterback Ron Jaworski said, "That's the greatest return I've ever seen in my life. It was the play of (that) year in the NFL. It's amazing!"

Even the members of the media broke out into applause, high-fiving each other in the Arrowhead Stadium press box.

After he crossed the goal line, Hall walked over to legendary Chiefs bandleader Tony DiPardo and handed him the ball.

# Best Buddies

Tony DiPardo
Photo courtesy of Scott E. Thomas Photography

*Tony DiPardo speaks about his relationship with Dante Hall.*

I keep asking myself one question. Why do all my dreams seem to come true? I never dreamed the most exciting player on the Kansas City Chiefs would become one of my best friends, but that's what happened back in 2002. Whether I am on the bandstand at Arrowhead Stadium or having dinner at a local restaurant, Chief fans keep coming up and asking me the same question. "DiPardo, how did you become such good friends with Dante Hall?" I love to answer it almost as much as I love Dante. He is the most special player I've met in all the years I've been associated with the Chiefs. I don't know why, or really how, our friendship got started, but it has grown and developed over the past few years to the point that I consider him a member of my family. Our friendship began in 2002 when the Chiefs played the St. Louis Rams. Anyone who has ever been to a Chiefs game, with little doubt, knows that I get very excited when the Chiefs score a touchdown or make a big play. But on this particular cold December afternoon, the old man got so excited that my toes tingled and the hair stood up on the back of my neck.

It was because Dante returned a kickoff 86 yards for a score. I was sitting in my director's chair with a Chiefs blanket over my legs just watching the play when, all of a sudden, Dante broke free, he crossed the end zone and ran right up to me and handed me the ball. I was so shocked! I couldn't believe it! I'd seen players spike the ball, slam it like a basketball over the goal post, toss it to some fans or hand it to an official, but never had I personally been on the receiving end of a getting a football after a touchdown. I didn't know what to say or do. I was speechless. I just stood there and looked up in the stands and all the fans were cheering. Of course they were cheering for Dante. But then, they began cheering for the old man, and I just felt so happy and excited. It was a feeling that started in my heart and then went through my body like a rocket. I showed the ball to my daughter, Patti, and we were hugging, and the guys in the band were giving me high-fives and I just couldn't stop thinking about Dante. Why on earth would someone like Dante Hall even think of an old guy like Tony DiPardo? I soon found out that Dante Hall knew more about me than I did about him. I didn't get the ball signed that day. I knew that Dante was going to be busy talking to all the reporters and I needed to get to another job that night. Christmas parties are big that time of year. So when I got home later that night, I put it on a shelf in my office. But I knew that I had to meet him soon and ask him why on earth he would do such a wonderful thing. I went to the stadium the next day and Dante was getting treatment. He came out and signed that ball and we sat and talked for the longest time. I knew we were going to be great friends. He told me I would need a trophy case for all the balls he was going to give me, and I built one. And it's filled with every touchdown return he had as a Chiefs player. It's like I said, I dream a lot. But I could never have dreamed about someone like Dante doing something this special for me.

*Dante Hall speaks about his relationship with Tony DiPardo.*

I didn't come to Kansas City looking for a 91-year-old friend. But I have one with Tony. I don't care if he's 91 or 191. He's my friend and he's one of the most special people in my life. I'm a guy who likes to do his research. When I got to Kansas City, I wanted to know everything about the community, about the team, about the fans – you name it, I found out about it. While I was doing that research, I kept reading the name Tony DiPardo. I asked people about him and I found out that he was much more than the Chiefs band leader. He'd played with Sammy Davis Jr., and he toured all over the country with his big band back in the hey-day of big band music during the '30s and '40s. He was a guy I wanted to meet, to talk with. And I thought to myself, "If I ever get the chance to meet him, we're going to hang (out) and talk music." When I ran that touchdown back against the Rams, I was heading into the end zone and I saw Tony. He was standing in front of the bandstand and his arms were up in the air like he was really cele-brating, really happy for me. It wasn't planned. I never thought about it once before the game or during the run, but I just ran over

> ❝ Why on earth would someone like Dante Hall even think of an old guy like Tony DiPardo? ❞

and handed him the ball. I could have given it to a fan, or saved it for myself, but I'll never forget the smile on his face when I gave it to him. I think he was about the happiest person I ever saw. When I saw how excited he was after I gave him that ball I made a vow to myself that every time I scored a touchdown, he was going to get the ball. I told him he was going to have to build a trophy case in his house for all the balls.

*Len Dawson, Chiefs Hall of Fame quarterback, talks about Dante's gift to Tony.*

Now you have to remember that I've known Tony for more than 40 years, and I could see how thrilled he was from way up in the press box. While I was broadcasting the game, I wondered why Dante would give Tony the ball. Like everyone else in the stadium, I wondered if they were good friends. I mean, talk about an odd couple – a 20-something kid from Texas and a 91-year-old Italian who is a Kansas City icon. After the game, I went down on the field to do my report and as I walked in the 50-yard line tunnel to the field, Tony was walking up from the field and he was holding that football like it was a newborn baby. I went up to him and said, 'Tony, I just talked to Dante and he wants that football back.' I was just joking, but the look of horror on Tony's face kind of scared me. I thought, "Oh, my God, I've caused Tony DiPardo to have a heart attack." I told him I was just kidding, and you could see the relief just wash over his entire body. He smiled and showed me the ball and told me that he was going to ask Dante to autograph it."

What do Raiders fans and laxatives have in common?

Both irritate the crap out of you.

# Famous Fans

Several VIPs are fans of the red-and-gold.

In this section, they describe what the Chiefs and game-day memories mean to them.

*"If you were throwing a football around in the backyard, you were Lenny the Cool – well, at least I was."*

I love going to Chiefs games. I've had season tickets for about as long as I can remember. Back when Neil Smith would do the baseball swing after a sack, and I found out he was doing that to honor me, that was pretty cool. A lot of guys like to go and stand on the sidelines to watch a game, and I've done that in the past, but my favorite way to experience a

Photo courtesy of Scott E. Thomas Photography

Chiefs game is to just go sit in my seats in the club level and yell and cheer just like any other fan. I played football in high school – which is no comparison to what these guys do – and I got to play a little quarterback at a workout in their indoor facility. I don't think until you see how big and fast and strong these guys are up close, you can begin to realize just how good they are.

**- GEORGE BRETT**
**Kansas City sports icon, Kansas City Royals and Pro Baseball Hall of Fame third baseman and longtime Chiefs season ticket holder.**

The coldest day of my life was at a Kansas City Chiefs game, and it wasn't just because of the cold weather. I know all Chiefs fans remember the Lin Elliott game – where he missed three field goals (of 35, 39, and 42 yards in a 10-7 home playoff loss to Indianapolis) that kept the team from advancing in the playoffs and probably going to the Super Bowl. When he missed each of those three

Frank White
Photo courtesy of Scott E. Thomas Photography

field goals, it just seemed to get colder and colder and colder. When it seemed like we had a chance to win the game, or at least tie it, you had this little feeling of warmth right here (pointing to his chest). Then, that cold came back following each missed field goal. I know the Colts fans weren't as cold as all of us Chiefs fans. I grew up in Kansas City, so I remember all the great Chiefs teams of the 1960s and early 1970s. Otis Taylor was my favorite player. The Joe Montana era was special, even though it just lasted a couple of years. It was fun watching Marcus Allen break all those touchdown records. How on earth did Oakland ever let him get away and come play in Kansas City?

**- FRANK WHITE**
**Kansas City native and Royals Hall of Fame second**
**baseman and eight-time Gold Glove winner.**

When I was a kid growing up in California, the Chiefs were the hip team. I really liked them. I saw them in the first Super Bowl and watched them win Super Bowl IV. They had the great linebackers – Jimmy Lynch, Bobby Bell, and Willie Lanier – the big offensive line, and

Kevin Costner & Stacy
Photo courtesy of Scott E. Thomas Photography

Lenny Dawson. Lenny the Cool – everyone wanted to be Lenny the Cool. If you were throwing a football around in the backyard, you were Lenny the Cool – well, at least I was. I had *Sports Illustrated* magazines with the Chiefs on the cover all over the walls of my room. When I was watching them play Cincinnati (a 27-20 Chiefs victory in the sixth game of the 2007 season) I noticed something. Cincinnati was trying to take out its toughest adversary first – Larry Johnson. You would see eight or nine guys in the box to stop Larry Johnson (who rushed for 119 yards) and they double-teamed Tony Gonzalez on every play. Since you asked, it did remind me of the final scene in "Open Range," where (my character) Charley Waite approaches a hired gun and asks, "You the one who killed our friend?" (The dapper villain smiles and spits out his final words: "I shot the boy, too, and I enjoyed it.") When I shot him, I was taking out my toughest adversary. It helped me out in the movie, but it didn't do much to help Cincinnati. The Chiefs didn't seem to have any problems at the line. Larry Johnson had a good game. You know, I can see why people like Kansas City. The stadium is great, the barbeque smells good and the grass is so green. Where I came from as a kid, if the grass was that green, there was a No Trespassing sign on it. And I've never seen as much red in my life as I saw at Arrowhead Stadium. Man, the fans love their team.

**- KEVIN COSTNER**

**Actor, writer, producer, director and star of such hits as *Open Range, Field of Dreams, Bull Durham* and the Academy Award winning *Dances with Wolves.***

Rick Sutcliffe
Photo courtesy of Scott E.
Thomas Photography

Have you ever been driving a car and felt two pairs of eyes from the back seat staring daggers into the back of your head? Well, I have. And let me tell you, it's not a very good feeling, especially after you're the one responsible for making your daughter and your best friend's son miss a game-winning field goal in the closing seconds of a game against the Denver Broncos.

I've had season tickets for as long as I can remember, and they're special to me and my family. My wife, Robin, used to mow yards to save up enough money so she and her dad could go see a Chiefs game. Since I do so much traveling for ESPN and other things, I try to catch as many Chiefs home games as possible. My best buddy, Rick Taylor, and his son, Ross, and my daughter, Shelby, picked me up at the airport back in 1997 to go see the Chiefs play the Broncos. That's one of those games you just never missed – especially back in the 1990s. I get off the plane, get in the car, and off we go to Arrowhead Stadium. Now, I've been to some games at Arrowhead that were cold, but this game was so cold I could hardly stand it. I wasn't dressed for the game, because I'd just gotten off that plane. It's kind of a back-and-forth game and by the end of the third quarter, I'm wondering if I'm going to make it through the whole game. The Broncos scored late and took a 22-21 lead and I told everyone we were leaving. Shelby and Ross kept saying, "What if they come back and win and we miss it?" I didn't care. I didn't think they were coming back and I couldn't feel my legs or my hands. I WAS COLD! So we get out in the parking lot and hear the crowd go crazy and I'm thinking to myself, if they come back and win this game I'm in trouble. We get in the car and hear the announcer say, "Stoyanovich is lining up for a 54-yard field goal." I'm thinking, if he makes it, this is going to be a long ride home. Well, he made it – and the glare from those four eyes sitting in the back seat just burned into the back of my head. Bill Grigsby gets on the radio and says, "I wonder what all those fans who left early are thinking?" Well, I can tell you what I was thinking – I'm never leaving a game early again. You know what? As long as that drive home was, I learned something that day and I think it helped me as a fan and a broadcaster. You really can't ever give up on a team. I doubt if we'd have left early if I hadn't been so cold, but I gave up on the team that day and I will never do it again – the Chiefs or any other team. I know one thing; the fans who stayed that day were sure rewarded. It must have been something else when that ball went through the uprights.

**- RICK SUTCLIFFE**
**Former Cy Young Award winner, present-day color analyst for ESPN baseball games, and a longtime Chiefs season ticket holder.**

I love football, especially game day at Arrowhead Stadium. I played professional baseball, but football is the sport I love. I love to watch it, and I almost played it in college. I've been to just about every NFL stadium in the country and I love Green Bay and Lambeau Field. It's like the home of football. But for a game-day experience, the tailgating, and enjoying a great experience, it's tough to beat Arrowhead Stadium.

**- BRIAN McRAE**
**Former all-state defensive back at Blue Springs High School and No. 1 draft pick of the Kansas City Royals, who went on to star for the Chicago Cubs and New York Mets.**

# Looking Ahead

In 2009, the Chiefs brought in a new general manager, a new coaching staff, and new hope for the future of the franchise.

Scott Pioli, Todd Haley, and the other newest members of the Chiefs family have plans to restore the glory!

# Plainly and Simply, A Football Guy

When Carl Peterson was announced as the new president, general manager and CEO of the Kansas City Chiefs in 1989, he was greeted with love and adoration by a hungry Chiefs Nation that was thirsty for success.

While the Chiefs became the winningest home franchise of the 1990s, fans soon became disillusioned with Peterson who said he had a "five-year plan" to get the team back into the playoffs and Super Bowl.

The team has not won a playoff game since 1993 and reached just one AFC title game – ironically, it came in that memorable 1993 season when Joe Montana and Marcus Allen looked like spry youngsters and nearly led the team to the promised land.

Peterson left the team following a disastrous 2-14 season in 2008 and his successor isn't about to make the same mistake of predicting when the team might enjoy postseason success.

"I don't think it's fair to set a timetable," new general manager Scott Pioli said when he was introduced to the Chiefs fans. "It's not about timing; it's about getting it right and this process is going to be very methodical, not just in where we're at with the coaching situation but where we're at with scouting and player personnel and the team. It takes time and I don't think it's fair to anybody to put time parameters on it right now."

While Peterson had his hand in all phases of the Chiefs day-to-day operations – and no one can argue with the success he had rebuilding the dwindling season-ticket base – Pioli is a football guy.

"The league is becoming increasingly complex in recent years," team owner Clark Hunt said. "It is no longer feasible for one person to effectively manage all aspects of an NFL franchise. Going forward, the general manager of the Kansas City Chiefs will be solely responsible for the football operation. As I have said from the outset, my ultimate goal is to build a team that can realistically aspire to win championships. I know championship teams are not built overnight. They are built through the draft and the draft process relies heavily on talent evaluation. To give it the best chance to be successful, we needed to hire the finest player personnel evaluator in the league, and I believe that we have done so with Scott Pioli."

Pioli teamed with coach Bill Belichick to help the New England Patriots win three Super Bowls and go 16-0 in the 2007 regular season. He was named the *Sporting News* NFL Executive of the Year following the 2003 and 2004 seasons; the youngest ever to receive the award, and one of only three NFL executives in history to win it in consecutive years.

**❝ It's not necessarily the best 53 players, it's the right 53 players. ❞**
*– New Chiefs GM Scott Pioli*

He is a mastermind when it comes to the draft, taking league MVP Tom Brady, and more recently the Defensive Rookie of the Year, Jerod Mayo. Of the 53 players on the Patriots Super Bowl XLII roster, 43 were acquired after the team's first championship in 2001. Thirty-one were acquired since the team's third title in 2004, demonstrating his ability to build a consistent winner.

And while the Chiefs have not won a playoff game since 1993, the Patriots have won 14 since 2000 – tying an NFL record for most playoff wins in a decade.

Pioli, who is not out-and-about town like Peterson so often was, said he is here to deliver a winning team.

"Here's what I believe: I believe that the main voice of the organization has to be the head coach," said Pioli, referring to the team's new head coach, Todd Haley. "The head coach is the leader of the football team that plays on Sunday. There will be times and places for me to be involved with the media."

When asked about his new team and its talent base, he said, simply, "I don't think it's fair for me to make a judgment until I know more about this football team. Until you're in the building and know the players and what they are, it's unfair to set any time frame. It's something you'll rarely hear from me. I don't think you're ever one or two players away. We're not building just for 2009. The goal is to build a team that has a long shelf life of being a good football team."

He is man who believes in piecing the right parts of the puzzle together to build a winner. That might not mean picking the most talented players, but the players who can fill a niche or a need.

"It's not necessarily the best 53 players, it's the right 53 players," he said. "It's bringing in football players who understand the culture that's been created or is being created. It's the personnel department and myself finding the players, knowing who the head coach is, what he is, what he stands for. Finding the players that can live within what the structure is going to be. What we will do is build a big, strong, fast, disciplined, smart football team. Those aren't just words. We will have smart football players, tough football players, mentally and physically. We will have disciplined football players and discipline has nothing to do with the length of their hair or how many gold chains they wear. Discipline has to do with being on time, working hard, and paying attention. That's the kind of staff we're going to have, what our entire football operation is going to be."

So why would a man with that type of passion come to a team that has not tasted postseason success for 15 years?

"There are professional reasons and there are personal reasons," he said. "I think we go through different seasons of life and different changes in life. I happen to be in one right now with a 5-year-old daughter and knowing where I'm going to be taking my family is very important to me. I can go anywhere and work and I'm going to be immersed in an environment where I'm taken care of. I think it's very important that I'm bringing my wife and daughter to a place that I know is going to be a good place for them, a place that's a wonderful place to raise our daughter. I know this community. My wife was born in Wichita and her mother's side of the family is from Wichita. A great deal of her family is still there and some in Kansas City. We have spent time in this area and we like the area and the community that we live in is very important to us. I'm giving you some of the personal reasons and we're looking forward to becoming part of this community."

And one can sense he looks even more forward to rebuilding a team like the one that ran roughshod over opponents throughout the 1990s.

"We saw the Chiefs early in the (2008) season," Pioli said, "And I know over the course of the season they went through a number of quarterbacks. They went through one of our quarterbacks. With the talent, obviously there needs to be some changes on the football team. With the way the team performed there needs to be changes. But I'll say this, though. Every season is different and every team regardless of the record is going to have natural attrition. There are going to be things that change on their own and things you need to change. There is going to be a transition."

# Out of the Darkness

Clark Hunt and Scott Pioli are on the same page.

That became evident when the Kansas City Chiefs owner and the new general manager began the search for a new head coach.

"Similar to the general manager search (that resulted in Pioli's hiring), we interviewed a broad and diverse group of candidates from around the league before arriving at our final decision," Hunt, the team owner, said. "As you know, Scott has a reputation for being extremely thorough when making player personnel decisions and he was just as thorough in his evaluation of each of the coaching candidates.

"As we began our search for the next head coach of the Chiefs there were a number of qualities that both Scott and I thought were important for a successful coach in the National Football League. We needed a head coach who was an excellent teacher, a strong leader and a good motivator to develop our young football team. We wanted a coach with a proven track record of success in building and coaching winning teams.

"It was also important for our head coach to have an understanding of the player personnel side of the operation and be able to effectively communicate his vision for the football team to the personnel department. Finally and most importantly, we were looking for a head coach who could partner with Scott to build the Chiefs into a championship organization."

Hunt and Pioli believe 41-year-old Todd Haley, the second-youngest coach in Chiefs history, can lead the team out of the darkness following a 2-14 season that claimed plenty of casualties.

"Todd is an outstanding football coach with a proven track record of success at every stop in his career, and we look forward to his leadership," Hunt said.

Added Pioli, "Having worked with Todd in New York from 1997-99 and having been mentored by some of the same people, we have a shared vision of what it takes to build a successful franchise in the National Football League. He will bring passion, dedication and energy to Kansas City, and I am confident that this is the beginning of a partnership that will serve the Chiefs well."

Haley was the offensive coordinator of the Phoenix Cardinals team that made such a dramatic run to the

Super Bowl in 2008-09, something Chiefs fans have not experienced since 1970.

"I am extremely excited and proud to be a part of the Kansas City Chiefs family and the Kansas City community," Haley said. "I am looking forward to working with Scott to re-establish the winning tradition that the tremendous fans in Kansas City deserve."

# There's Nothing Trivial about the Chiefs' New QB

Matt Cassel is the answer to a pretty impressive trivia question.

According to the research team at ESPN, he is the only quarterback in the history of the NFL to start a game without having started a game in college.

While playing at USC, the new Kansas City Chiefs signal caller was a backup to a couple of Heisman Trophy winners in Carson Palmer and Matt Leinart. After a strong showing at the NFL Combine, the New England Patriots selected Cassel in the seventh round of the 2005 NFL draft.

He started his NFL career as a backup to Super Bowl hero Tom Brady and veteran Doug Flutie, but in an O. Henryish twist to his career that drips with irony, he earned a starting job thanks to his present-day teammate, Kansas City safety Bernard Pollard.

Pollard knocked the league's reigning MVP, Brady, out for the season in the opening game of the 2008 season. Brady's knee injury opened the door for Cassel.

He came in and led the Patriots to a 17-10 victory over the Chiefs and finished the season in impressive fashion – completing 327 of 516 passes for 3,946 yards and 23 touchdowns.

The Patriots slapped their franchise tag on the hottest young commodity in the league in February 2009 and then promptly traded him to the Chiefs, when the Patriots found out Brady's knee was healthy and that the NFL poster boy would return in 2009.

The Chiefs' 2009 season marks the first year since Cassel was in high school that he will begin the season as his team's starting quarterback.

"I am really excited about it," Cassel said. "I am excited about the opportunity. I was here in 2005 and know how excited the city is about its team and how excited the fans get at Arrowhead Stadium."

When asked if he had met Pollard to thank him, Cassel just grinned.

"I will talk with him and thank him for the opportunity, but we all know (the hit) wasn't intentional. No one likes to see anyone go down with an injury. But I am thankful for this opportunity."

And he's making the most of this opportunity.

"Slowly but surely, this is beginning to feel like my team," he said. "Like anything, everything's new to me. It's a new environment. It's new teammates. I'm getting to know the receivers, getting to know my linemen and my running backs and we're progressing.

"There's no doubt about that. We're getting better each and every practice I'm out there and it's a new playbook as well for me. So, I'm sharpening up my reads each and every day, I'm working hard and that's all I can do. I can go out and do what I can do, control what I can control and try to perform out there every day I get an opportunity to."

Cassel believes the past has toughened him up and made him ready for finally being a starter.

"It's one of those things, you get toughened up by everything that goes on, overcoming a lot of adversity. You know what I mean? There's going to be adversity that comes up during the season whether we lose a game or whether it's a tough play or an interception or something like that. You just always have to be able to overcome it and be mentally tough. I think throughout the years you continue to be mentally tough and you continue to push through and know that there is a bright spot at the end of the tunnel."

After each day of practice, Cassel notices that he's earning the trust and respect of his new teammates.

"Each and every day you just go out there and you try to build on stuff," he said.

"Whether it's working on a route, whether it's a certain play, whether it's a concept you want to see. It's just building that rapport. That's something that comes with time. That's all it is. It's repetition and time."

With a new team, a new coach and a new outlook on his NFL career, Cassel can't wait for the season to begin.

He knows this is his best shot to win a job since his prep days.

"Are you kidding me?" he asked, laughing. "Against Brady last year? They totally gave me a shot. They were like 'it was me – Brady,' juggling it.

"It's great to be with the Chiefs because you get an opportunity to go out there and get the first-team reps and really get to start building that relationship with the receivers.

"I think any time you're a backup quarterback and have to step into that role, it took me a little time last year to get on the same page with those guys because you just don't get those reps. But right now, it's so valuable to be out there and be with the ones and be able to get those reps and see the defense and go against the number one defense because they're doing a great job out there and they're getting a lot better, as well."

Haley calls his new quarterback a "gym rat."

Cassel takes that as a compliment.

"I've had an opportunity to really learn behind one of the best, which is Tom. I credit a lot of my work ethic and what I do off the field to what he's been able to teach me and really how to be a professional. He's a professional in every sense of the word. I was lucky enough, like I said, to kind of learn the work ethic, how to be a professional, how to study and do those things that I need to do to make myself the best on Sundays. But, at the same time, I've always had a work ethic of the utmost. I love to go out, I love to be in the gym, I love to work out and that just carries over."

# Authors

**Bill Althaus** is an award-winning columnist for The Examiner in eastern Jackson County, Missouri. The Simone Award Committee named him the media personality of the year in 2006 and presented him with the Gordon Docking Award. He followed that honor with the Morris Excellence in Journalism Award in 2007. The Independence, Missouri, native has also been honored by the Missouri Press Association, the *Associated Press* and *United Press International*. This is his fourth book featuring the franchise and members of the Kansas City Chiefs, including Priest Holmes, Dante Hall and legendary Kansas City icon Tony DiPardo. Bill and his wife, Stacy, have two sons – Zach, a graduate of Rockhurst University, and Sean, a college sophomore.

**Rich Wolfe**'s books have sold well over a million copies in the United States. Wolfe has authored the best-selling books in the history of Notre Dame and the Chicago Cubs. The Iowa native is the only person to appear on both *Jeopardy!* and ESPN's *Two-Minute Drill*. In 2006, he was inducted as one of Leahy's Lads at Notre Dame.